Perspective Criticism

PERSPECTIVE CRITICISM

Point of View and Evaluative Guidance
in Biblical Narrative

Gary Yamasaki

CASCADE *Books* · Eugene, Oregon

PERSPECTIVE CRITICISM
Point of View and Evaluative Guidance in Biblical Narrative

Copyright © 2012 Gary Yamasaki. All rights reserved. Except for brief quotations in critical publications or reviews, no part of this book may be reproduced in any manner without prior written permission from the publisher. Write: Permissions, Wipf and Stock Publishers, 199 W. 8th Ave., Suite 3, Eugene, OR 97401.

Cascade Books
An Imprint of Wipf and Stock Publishers
199 W. 8th Ave., Suite 3
Eugene, OR 97401

www.wipfandstock.com

ISBN 13: 978-1-62032-583-4

Cataloguing-in-Publication data:

Yamasaki, Gary.

Perspective criticism : point of view and evaluative guidance in biblical narrative / Gary Yamasaki.

viii + 164 pp. ; 23 cm. Includes bibliographical references and indexes.

ISBN 13: 978-1-62032-583-4

1. Bible—Criticism, Narrative. 2. Perspective (Linguistics). 3. Narration (Rhetoric). I. Title.

BS521.7 Y36 2012

Manufactured in the U.S.A.

Revised Standard Version of the Bible, copyright © 1952 [2nd edition, 1971] by the Division of Christian Education of the National Council of the Churches of Christ in the United States of America. Used by permission. All rights reserved.

To April,

... my inspiration

Contents

1. Point-of-View Crafting: An Untapped Source of Evaluative Guidance · 1
2. Spatial Plane of Point of View · 18
3. Psychological Plane of Point of View · 35
4. Informational Plane of Point of View · 54
5. Temporal Plane of Point of View · 69
6. Phraseological Plane of Point of View · 91
7. Ideological Plane of Point of View · 98
8. When the Planes Concur . . . and When They Do Not · 106
9. A Perspective-Critical Analysis of the Butch Cassidy Clip · 117
10. New Testament Case Study: Gamaliel (Acts 5:35–39) · 128
11. Old Testament Case Study: Gideon (Judges 6:36–40) · 140

Bibliography · 155

Scripture Index · 159

Movie Index · 163

one

Point-of-View Crafting
An Untapped Source of Evaluative Guidance

You are proceeding through the book of Judges and, in chapter 6, you encounter a new character, Gideon. You see him being commissioned by an angel of the Lord to deliver the Israelites out of the hands of the Midianites. You sense a hero in the making as he follows the Lord's leading in destroying an altar of pagan worship and replacing it with an altar to the Lord. But, you also sense a tentativeness about him, for he is only willing to follow the Lord's leading during the night, when no one is watching.

At the end of the chapter, you see him using pieces of fleece as a means of determining from the Lord whether Israel will indeed prevail over the Midianites in battle, and you wonder about this. Are Gideon's actions with the fleece to be taken positively—as a model for discerning God's will—or are they to be taken negatively—as a show of distrust in God's original instructions? You glance over at the storyteller, but he's not telling.

THIS IS A PREDICAMENT faced countless times by readers of the Bible—the report of a character engaged in some action, but no explicit indication from the storyteller on how the action is to be evaluated. At first glance, it would appear the readers are being left to fend for themselves in making an evaluation. Fortunately, that is not the case, for though the readers are not receiving explicit evaluative guidance, they may be receiving guidance in a less-obvious fashion through the way in which *point of view* is being used in the passage.

Perspective Criticism

The present work sets out a new biblical methodology called *Perspective Criticism*, an approach designed to uncover evaluative guidance that may be encoded in the point-of-view crafting of biblical narratives.[1] This first chapter unpacks the literary concept of point of view—a concept that defies simple explanation—and also describes how point-of-view crafting can be used to provide evaluative guidance in a narrative text. This provides a foundation for the comprehensive look into the details of point-of-view crafting in the chapters that follow.

As you glance back at the storyteller, you notice that though he is not telling you whether or not you should be siding with Gideon, he is giving you a wink and a nod. He is indeed providing you with signals as to his evaluative intentions. It's just going to take some digging to learn how to interpret the signals.

Narrator as Story-World Tour Guide

Gaining a grasp of the literary concept of point of view requires first becoming acquainted with another concept foreign to the conventional historical approach to biblical studies, that is, the concept of a story's *narrator*. When conceptualizing readers reading a biblical story, it is most natural to envision them simply receiving the words of the story from the author. However, according to literary theory,[2] the words are not being communicated directly from author to reader. Rather, the author is understood as creating a voice that speaks the words of the story to the reader, and this voice is known as the narrator.

For the purposes of gaining a grasp of this concept, it is most helpful to turn to the genre of film. Consider the opening of the cult classic *The Gods Must Be Crazy* (1980). The first sixteen minutes of the movie set the stage for a story line involving Xi, a member of the Sho people indigenous to the Kalahari Desert of Botswana, and his dealings with a Coke bottle dropped by a passing aircraft. This opening portion of the movie first provides a brief introduction to the Kalahari Desert, then turns to life among

---

1. For a comprehensive treatment of the theoretical background to this methodology, see Yamasaki, *Watching*, 1–67.

2. It is important to make clear at the outset that the literary methodology developed in the present work belongs to the text-oriented approach to literary studies reflected in the New Criticism of the mid-twentieth century whose focus is the response of the reader *presupposed* by the text, and not the more recent reader-oriented post-structuralist approaches whose focus is the response of actual real-life readers.

the Sho people—contrasting it with life in urban South Africa—and then turns to Xi's discovery of the Coke bottle and the strife it causes within his family, leading him to conclude it is evil and should be thrown off the end of the earth.

What distinguishes these scenes from most other filmmaking is the presence of a male voice speaking over the images on the screen. This is a *narrator* providing commentary on what the audience is seeing. For example, in the section covering life in urban South Africa,[3] the camera gives a close-up of an old-style digital clock flipping from 7:29 to 7:30, and then cuts to a car pulling out of a driveway and starting down the street, as the voice-over reports, "If the day is called 'Monday' and the number 'seven-three-zero' comes up, you have to disadapt yourself from your domestic surroundings and readapt yourself to an entirely different environment." Then, after nine seconds of various shots of the morning rush hour, the camera settles on an outdoor digital clock switching from 7:59 to 8:00, and then cuts to a shot of office workers settling in for the day's work, as the voice-over says, "'Eight-double zero' means everybody has to look busy." There are then short shots of an executive sitting down at his desk and an auto worker plying his trade, followed by a longer thirteen-second shot of a journalist named Kate saying on the phone, "I've got a very good story here about handicapped children . . ." but then having to hold the receiver away from her ear because of yelling on the other end. Then she continues, "All right. Look, I'm sorry. I'll print only sweetness and light even if it bores the pants off people."

Here, the camera cuts to a digital clock displaying 10:30, and then provides short shots of the executive receiving a cup of coffee from his assistant and a group of auto workers guzzling soft drinks, with the voice-over saying, "'Ten-three-zero' says you can stop looking busy for fifteen minutes . . ." Then the clock is shown flipping from 10:44 to 10:45, and the voice-over continues ". . . and then you have to look busy again" with the camera cutting to a short shot of one of the auto workers with a welding torch, and then to a longer seventeen-second shot of Kate as she is approached by Pete, a co-worker, who hands her some papers and says, "Do you think you could use this? It's about the shortage of teachers in Botswana." She responds, "Good story?" and he says, "Yah, they're so short they'll take anyone who can read and write." After glancing over the sheets, she replies, "I don't know. I got bawled out for writing a story on mugging. He said my

---

3. At 6:40—8:13.

page should only have sweetness and light, like Liberace and Jackie Onassis . . . I'm sorry."

The camera then cuts to a digital clock displaying 1:00:00, followed by a short shot of two businessmen having lunch, as the voice-over comments, "And so your day is chopped up into little pieces, and in each segment of time, you have to adapt to a new set of circumstances," finishing just as Kate is shown in a cafeteria asking if she can share a table with a woman already seated. She sits down, with the voice-over continuing, "No wonder some people go off the rails a bit" and the scene continues with the other woman looking over at her, and saying, "Does the sound in my head bother you?" to which Kate gives a wary "No" and turns away. The camera then cuts to Kate back at the office seeking out Pete, and saying, "Have you still got that story about the teacher shortage in Botswana?" Pete replies, "Yah, you gonna use it?" to which Kate responds, "No, but maybe they could use me."

The camera then cuts to the Kalahari Desert to show Xi walking through the grasslands, and the voice-over says, "But in the Kalahari, it's always Tuesday or Thursday, if you like . . . or Sunday. No clocks or calendars to tell you to do this or that."[4]

The narrator voice heard over the video of this clip is not that of the author of the screenplay, Jamie Uys. Rather, it is a voice created by Uys for the purpose of conveying comments to the audience on what is being shown on the screen, and this illustrates what literary theory understands all written narratives to have: just such a voice making comments to readers. However, literary theory would understand the narrator of a written narrative as having a much more extensive role than the one this movie narrator plays. In the one-minute forty-three second clip covered above, the narrator is speaking for only thirty seconds, meaning the audience is receiving only a fraction of the cinematic data from this source, with the visual images and the audio sounds supplying the bulk of the data. In contrast, the narrator of a written narrative is involved during 100 percent of the story, as every word of every sentence in the whole story is spoken by the narrator to the readers. Further, a written narrative has no images on a screen and no audio soundtrack, and so, the readers receive 100 percent of the story data from the narrator's words.

The all-encompassing control of story data by narrators of written stories is better illustrated by the opening scene of *Stranger Than Fiction*

---

4. At 8:13—8:23.

Point-of-View Crafting

(2006),[5] the story of a man who discovers he is a character in a novel-in-progress who is slated to be killed off by the end of the novel. The opening scene begins with a zooming in—from a point in outer space right down to a close-up of a wristwatch on a bedside table—at which point a woman's voice is heard, saying, "This is a story about a man named Harold Crick . . . and his wristwatch." The camera then cuts to a man lying in bed, as the voice-over continues, "Harold Crick was a man of infinite numbers, endless calculations, and remarkably few words . . ." And as the camera zooms in on his hand reaching to turn off the alarm on his watch, the voice-over adds, ". . . and his wristwatch said even less."

The camera then cuts to Harold brushing his teeth, and the voice-over continues, "Every weekday for twelve years, Harold would brush each of his thirty-two teeth seventy-six times . . . thirty-eight times back and forth . . . thirty-eight times up and down." The camera then cuts to Harold tying his tie, and the voice-over continues, "Every weekday for twelve years, Harold would tie his tie in a single Windsor knot, instead of the double, thereby saving up to forty-three seconds. His wristwatch thought the single Windsor made his neck look fat . . . but said nothing." And the voice-over continues on for nearly two more minutes, making comments as the camera follows Harold going to work, engaging in his job at an IRS office, eating his lunch, taking a coffee break, walking from the bus stop to his home, eating supper, and going to bed.

The voice-over addresses practically everything the audience sees on the screen, providing so much information the audience could conceivably follow the story even without the benefit of the images on the screen. This clip from *Stranger Than Fiction* provides a closer analogy to a narrator's work in a written narrative, for similar to the voice-over in this clip, the narrator of a written narrative is constantly speaking,[6] conveying sentence after sentence of text to the readers.

In a sense, the narrator functions as a tour guide of the story world, with the words of the narrator serving up for the readers descriptions of characters engaged in actions within the confines of the story world. It is important to note, however, a narrator will not usually be a benign tour guide, simply passing on information to the readers in an objective manner.

---

5. At 0:40—3:44.

6 The analogy is not perfect; while the voice-over in the *Stranger Than Fiction* clip is very prominent, it does fall silent three times for periods of nine, sixteen, and nine seconds, whereas the narrator of a written narrative never falls silent.

Rather, a narrator is apt to steer the readers into having particular stances on the actions they witness while touring around in the story world.

This type of evaluative steering is evident in the clip from *The Gods Must Be Crazy* covered earlier. Though the narrator does not explicitly criticize the way in which members of urban South-African culture are bound by the clock and calendar, it is clear he is steering his audience to disapprove of such a lifestyle. So, here is another important component of the job of a narrator: to provide evaluative guidance for the readers.

This is true of all narrators, including biblical narrators. The narrators of the Bible narratives are not content if their readers simply gain awareness of the events recorded; rather, they want to ensure their readers come away from these stories with particular evaluative stances on the events experienced. The most obvious means for providing evaluative guidance is the inclusion of explicit evaluative comments on the events in the story world. An example of this can be found in 1 Kgs 11:6 where, in his coverage of Solomon's marriages to many foreign women, the narrator of the book of Kings notes, "So Solomon did evil in the eyes of the Lord," a piece of commentary making clear to the readers how they are to evaluate Solomon's actions. And this is just one in a series of explicit evaluative comments made by the narrator of Kings on the kings of Judah and Israel.

It should be noted the work of the narrator of Kings is not indicative of the practices of biblical narrators in general, for explicit evaluative commentary like this is used only sparingly in the rest of the narrative books of the Bible. However, this paucity of explicit evaluative commentary does not mean readers of biblical texts are left without any guidance on how they are to evaluate the actions of biblical characters. Biblical storytellers do have at their disposal more subtle means for getting their evaluative stances across to their audiences, and these are the preferred means for most biblical narrators. Meir Sternberg provides a concise survey of the variety of ways biblical narrators exercise the art of persuasion on their audiences.[7] One of the fifteen techniques he treats is point-of-view manipulation but, unfortunately, he only addresses a fraction of the persuasive power inherent in point-of-view dynamics. The remainder of this chapter will demonstrate how point-of-view manipulation is perhaps a narrator's most powerful and most versatile tool for impacting an audience's evaluation of characters in a story.

---

7. Sternberg, *Poetics*, 475–81.

The Functioning of Point of View in a Narrative

Point of view is a literary concept developed in the study of the modern novel beginning in the late nineteenth century, and even held the distinction of being the most prominent topic of discussion in literary circles during the twentieth century. Outside literary circles, however, point of view is not well understood. Therefore, considerable space will be devoted to unpacking this literary concept.

In the field of literary criticism, the most often quoted definition of point of view is that of literary critic Percy Lubbock: "The whole intricate question of method, in the craft of fiction, I take to be governed by the question of the point of view—the question of the relation in which the narrator stands to the story."[8] This dictum clearly reflects the place of prominence held by the concept of point of view, but Lubbock's actual definition of point of view—"the relation in which the narrator stands to the story"—is anything but illuminating, and thus, requires further attention.

As mentioned earlier, the function of a narrator is to act as something akin to a tour guide, and this involves positioning the readers at various vantage points within the story world of a narrative. To visualize this dynamic, it is helpful to think of how a film director uses the positioning of a movie camera to set the viewers at a certain vantage point in the film's story world;[9] to put it another way, the director gives the audience the illusion of standing in the exact spot occupied by the movie camera, having the audience view the rest of the story world from that spot.

Particularly instructive in this regard is a sequence from the movie *The Truman Show* (1998), the account of a man who, unbeknownst to him, has been the subject of a television show his entire life, his every move being captured by hundreds of cameras hidden throughout his hometown, which is actually nothing more than an elaborate filming set. The sequence is from a part of the storyline where Truman is becoming obsessed with the possibility that things are not what they seem,[10] precipitated by him catching a glimpse of a man whom Truman thinks is his long-dead father. Christof, the show's creator and director, wants to distract Truman from

---

8. Lubbock, *Craft of Fiction*, 251.

9. The first biblical scholar to appeal to the analogy of the use of movie cameras to explain the workings of point of view was Adele Berlin, "Point of View," 71–73.

10. At 58:39—1:00:23.

Perspective Criticism

this obsession, and so, orchestrates a meeting between him and the actor who had been written out of the script twenty-three years earlier.

Leading up to the sequence in question, Truman and his best friend Marlon are shown sitting at the end of an unfinished bridge talking about Truman's growing suspicions there is something going on. During the conversation, Truman's attention is drawn to a shadowy figure approaching along the bridge deck. As Truman starts toward the figure, the camera cuts to Christof in his control center, which is equipped with a number of video monitors, each connected to a different camera planted in various places on, and around, the bridge. Christof is shown calling for the "CraneCam," at which point there appears on the monitor in front of him a high angle shot from behind Truman. As the two men are about to meet, Christof calls for "ButtonCam 3" at which point the monitor shows a frontal shot of Truman from just a few feet away, but shooting up from waist height. Then Christof calls for "CurbCam 8" at which point there appears on the monitor a shot showing the two men in profile from about fifteen feet away. And, as the two men embrace, Christof says, ". . . and now, go in close . . ." at which point the image on the monitor switches to a high-angle medium shot, with the camera slowly zooming in on Truman's face.

For each segment of this sequence, Christof dictates which camera feed is to be used, and in so doing, he dictates the particular angle from which the members of his audience view the segment. He is, in essence, placing them in various positions within his story world—vantage points from which they watch the action: first, high up and behind Truman, and then, at waist level looking up at his face, and then, at curb height fifteen feet away, and then, up and off to the side, but slowing descending upon Truman.

This provides an apt illustration of what is at the root of point of view in written narratives. In the same way a filmmaker determines the angle from which the audience is to view any particular segment of a scene, so also, a narrator in a written narrative places the readers in a specific position within the story world to facilitate their watching the action of a given segment of the narrative from a particular angle.

This assertion raises two issues. First, how is it possible to conceive of readers as *watching* the action of a story? Unlike moviegoers who are presented with images on a screen, readers have only words on a page at which to look. Therefore, how is it possible to conceive of readers being engaged in the act of *watching*? The answer to this question is to be found

Point-of-View Crafting

in another look at the activity of the narrator. Earlier, a narrator was likened to a tour guide leading readers through a story world. To expand upon this, part of a narrator's guidance is the provision of descriptions of elements of the story world—descriptions of people, events, and places—and these descriptions create *images* for the readers to view. Of course, the readers have no screen on which to view these images. Rather, they view them in their *mind's eye*; the act of reading involves something akin to watching a movie unfold inside one's head. So, it is indeed conceivable that readers *watch* the action of a written narrative.

There is still, however, a second issue. Even if it is conceded that readers do *watch* the action of a story, is it really possible readers can be positioned, simply by words in a text, to watch the action *from a particular angle*? This issue is best addressed by means of an exercise in visualization. First, read the following account of Jesus' ascension from Luke 24:51, visualizing in your mind these events as you read: "And while Jesus was blessing them, he parted from them and was carried up into heaven."[11] Now, compare what you have visualized with the way in which the *Jesus Film* (1979) portrays these events.[12] It starts with a close-up of Jesus in semi-profile speaking words of blessing, and with his voice continuing, the camera cuts to a shot of his followers looking off-camera to the left, then kneeling and raising their arms, with their gaze shifting upward toward the sky. Then the camera cuts to an aerial shot looking down on the followers with the camera rising, resulting in the followers on the ground looking smaller and smaller.

No one would visualize this when reading Luke 24:51. Rather, a person engaging in this exercise will typically visualize a shot from the ground looking up at the ascending Jesus. For what reason? The linguistics of this verse dictate a viewing angle from the ground looking up, with a viewing angle from the sky looking down requiring different linguistics.

Linguistics can play a significant role in dictating the angle from which readers view a particular scene in their mind's eye. This being the case, it is often possible to determine from a linguistic analysis of a narrative passage that the readers are intended to view the action described from one angle as opposed to another. Having said that, it is important to point out linguistics do not have the capacity to dictate viewing angles with the fine gradations possible with the adjustments to the positioning of a movie camera. Nevertheless, linguistics do have the capacity to dictate viewing

11. All translations are the author's own, unless otherwise indicated.
12. At 1:53:29—1:54:00.

angles to a degree sufficient to make significant differences to the readers' experience of a narrative.

The discussion of point of view to this point has relied heavily on the analogy of how the positioning of a movie camera dictates the angles from which an audience views the action of a movie. However, this analogy needs to be supplemented, for when it comes to point of view in a written narrative, talk of the spatial positioning of readers in a narrative's story world only scratches the surface of the full extent of the narrative's point-of-view dynamics. We will be exploring the components contributing to this full extent of point-of-view dynamics in the following several chapters. However, it is helpful at this point to take a step back and have a look at the big picture of point-of-view crafting, that is, the end toward which the various components of point-of-view manipulation work. Put simply, that end is providing the readers with either a *subjective* or *objective* experience of particular elements of a story. In other words, the point-of-view crafting of a narrative text is analyzed to determine if the readers are being led to merge with a given character, thus experiencing the action subjectively along with the character, or if they are being held at arm's length from the character, thus experiencing the character's participation in the action as mere objective bystanders.

Analysis of point of view to the degree being suggested here constitutes uncharted territory in the field of biblical studies. However, it remains to be determined whether or not it is territory worth charting. Until recently, scholarship on point of view had failed to uncover any way in which awareness of the point-of-view crafting in a biblical narrative makes a significant impact on how the narrative is interpreted. However, the uncovering of a relatively obscure aspect of the point-of-view theory developed in the study of the modern novel provides the key for developing a methodology for analyzing point of view that does indeed impact biblical interpretation. It is to this aspect of point-of-view theory that we now turn.

THE EXEGETICAL SIGNIFICANCE OF POINT OF VIEW

The bulk of the efforts by biblical scholars in working with point of view has focused on a few standard works of literary criticism known for their treatments of this literary concept.[13] Unfortunately, none of these

---

13. For an assessment of these efforts by New Testament and Old Testament narrative critics, see Yamasaki, *Watching*, 68–151.

standard works address how being aware of the point-of-view dynamics in a narrative text can actually impact the interpretation of the text, with the one point-of-view dynamic that does prove significant in this regard laying hidden away in a prominent literary-critical work of the early-1960s not ordinarily associated with the concept of point of view.

The work in question is *The Rhetoric of Fiction*, written by American literary critic Wayne Booth,[14] and his contribution to point-of-view theory is found in a provocative analysis of Jane Austen's *Emma*.[15] The title character of this novel is a young woman who is intelligent, witty, beautiful, and wealthy. However, she also cannot keep herself from meddling in the affairs of others, often to their extreme detriment. Booth discerns that Austen's composing of this story is governed by two basic interests. On the one hand, she wants the story to be a comedy, and on the other, she wants the audience to wish for Emma's happiness in the end. Further, Booth notes these two interests are at odds with each other, for while Emma's ill-informed meddling is essential as the source of much of the comedy of the story, its devastating results for those around her have the natural effect of turning the readers against her as opposed to having them wish for her happiness. Therefore, Austen's challenge is to retain the meddling, but in such a way as to keep the audience from becoming distanced from Emma.

Booth convincingly argues that Austen meets this challenge through an ingenious use of point of view, specifically, "showing most of the story through Emma's eyes,"[16] that is, through Emma's point of view. According to Booth, this dynamic creates within the readers a sense of *empathy* for Emma despite all her misdeeds, and this feeling of empathy results in the readers pulling for her in the end.

This finding by Booth has made virtually no impact on the study of point of view in biblical narratives; the only biblical scholar to note this dynamic has been Janice Capel Anderson, and she only mentions it in passing.[17] This lack of attention from biblical narrative critics is unfortunate, for Booth's discovery has profound significance for the analysis of biblical narratives. As mentioned earlier, biblical narrators use evaluative commentary

---

14. Booth, *Rhetoric*; the first edition was published in 1961, but all page references are to the second edition (1983).

15. Ibid., 243–66.

16. Ibid., 245.

17. Anderson, *Narrative Web*, 67, bringing up a point she made in an unpublished paper from 1981.

only sparingly, thus leaving their readers without explicit guidance on whether they are to approve or disapprove of the vast majority of actions they witness. However, Booth's discovery means even in a narrative text containing no explicit evaluative commentary, *evaluative guidance may still be present in the point-of-view crafting of the text*. Specifically, filtering the events of the story line through a particular character's point of view creates within the readers a sense of empathy for the character and, as a result, the readers will be inclined to side with the character in whatever he or she does; in other words, the readers are led to evaluate the character's actions positively.

The idea that readers should feel empathy for a character through whose point of view they are experiencing a story is nothing new. It has long been recognized that characters functioning as first-person narrators draw the empathy of their readers. First-person narration involves every aspect of a story coming to the readers through the point of view of the narrator-character, a dynamic resulting in an intimacy between readers and character as the readers' experience of the story comes to merge with that character's experience. And the natural outcome of such a merging is the readers develop a sense of empathy with the character.

What is ground-breaking about Booth's finding is that this sense of empathy could occur where the narration is not being presented with the intimacy of a first-person narrator, but rather, with the distance of a third-person narrator—a narrator who is not involved as a character in the story, but rather, is relating the story as an uninvolved bystander. However, despite the fact the readers feel a sense of distance from the narrator, a sense of intimacy can still be created *with one of the characters*. This can occur when the aspects of the story are relayed to the readers *through the point of view of that character,* such that the readers' experience of the events merges with the character's experience, with this merging producing within the readers a sense of empathy with the character.

Therefore, taking the scenario that opened this chapter—a reader, with no explicit evaluative commentary on which to rely, wondering whether to approve or disapprove of Gideon's actions with the fleece—a perspective-critical analysis would examine this passage from Judges for the point-of-view moves used in its crafting to determine whether they serve to lead the readers to experience the events of the story line through Gideon's point of view. If so, the resulting merging of the readers with Gideon has the effect of having them empathize with him, and thus approve of his actions.

Point-of-View Crafting

The Hebrew Scriptures are replete with situations such as this—passages involving dubious actions, but lacking explicit evaluative commentary—constituting a sizeable corpus ripe for the investigative power of perspective criticism. Further, this methodology should be equally helpful in discerning evaluative guidance in biblical stories involving controversies between characters where, again, the narrator does not explicitly indicate with which of the characters the readers are to side.

For example, in Acts 15:36–40, Paul and Barnabas are about to embark on a second missionary journey, but they end up in a sharp disagreement over whether or not to take John Mark along, with Barnabas thinking they should, but Paul insisting they do not. In fact, their disagreement becomes so sharp they end up splitting as a team. Obviously, one of them is missing the mark here, but the narrator does not indicate explicitly which one that is. However, if a perspective-critical analysis of the point-of-view dynamics of this passage reveals the report of this event is being filtered through the point of view of one of these characters, it can be concluded the readers are intended to side with that character.

The proposal presented here—that something as seemingly innocuous as point-of-view crafting has the capacity to dictate the characters with whom the readers are to empathize—is radical indeed. And it may be objected that perhaps too much is being made of Booth's study of *Emma*. However, the "anti-hero" genre of literature and film stands as corroborating evidence of the veracity of this empathy dynamic. Stories of this genre utilize protagonists who exhibit characteristics traditionally associated with villains rather than heroes. While such characterizations would ordinarily function to distance audiences from such characters, no such distance arises in the case of anti-heroes. In fact, the opposite occurs; audiences find themselves siding with such characters, pulling for them in whatever they do. And this sense of empathy for anti-heroes results from point-of-view manipulation designed to have the events of the story filtered through the point of view of such characters—establishing them as the "point-of-view characters" of their respective stories—resulting in audiences coming to side with them.

A clip from the classic anti-hero film *Butch Cassidy and the Sundance Kid* (1969) demonstrates this empathy dynamic in action. The title characters are members of a gang of outlaws in the Wild West of the 1890s, and during the first thirty-five minutes of the movie, they are depicted as being of corrupt character—planning a bank job, cheating at cards, pulling

Perspective Criticism

off train robberies—behavior not surprising for the outlaws they are. At around the thirty-five minute mark, one of their train robberies is interrupted by the arrival of a posse, initiating a chase sequence that goes on for the next twenty-five minutes. Space does not permit coverage of the whole chase sequence, but examination of a representative clip of the sequence should suffice for our purposes.[18]

The clip opens with a short shot of Butch and Sundance on a horse at full gallop, traversing a wide-open area of desert conditions, and then cuts to Butch letting himself flop into a pool of water on a rocky plateau. As he cools off in the pool, he calls out to an off-camera Sundance, "Ah, you're wasting your time . . ." The camera then pulls back to focus on Sundance in the foreground kneeling by the edge of the plateau, as Butch continues talking in the background, ". . . can't track us over rock." Sundance, apparently spotting something in the distance, leans forward and says, "Tell *them* that."

Butch, stunned at the implications of what Sundance has just said, clambers out of the pool, and sloshes over toward Sundance, coming to settle in beside him, peering off in the same direction. The camera then cuts to a shot of the posse members in the distance on a rocky expanse below, and then returns to Butch and Sundance still staring in their direction. Butch then says, "They're beginning to get on my nerves . . . who are those guys?" In response, Sundance recounts an incident years earlier where they were told of "a full-blooded Indian, except he called himself with an English name, 'Sir . . . somebody . . .'" Butch interjects, "Lord Baltimore?" and then Sundance says, "Lord Baltimore, that's right. And he could track anybody, over anything, day or night." Butch, not catching the significance, simply replies, "So?" Sundance continues, "The guy on the ground . . . I think it's him." The camera cuts back to the posse in the distance, five of the riders still mounted, and one off his horse and examining something on the ground. The camera then cuts back to Butch and Sundance, Butch saying, "No, Baltimore works out of Oklahoma . . . he's strictly an Oklahoma man," and after glancing around, adds, "I don't know where we are, but it sure as hell isn't Oklahoma." Then, after a few moments of exchanging reassurances—reassurances that ring hollow under these new circumstances—Sundance gets up to depart, leaving Butch with his eyes still fixed on the posse. The camera then cuts back to the posse in the distance for a few more seconds.

---

18. At 51:02—58:12.

Point-of-View Crafting

The next scene opens with a couple of shots of Butch and Sundance riding down the middle of a creek, and then veering out of the water, dismounting, and starting up the base of a mountain, with their horse in tow. The camera then cuts to a high-angle shot down on the creek below, capturing Butch in the foreground stopping, looking back, and exclaiming, "Damn it!" As Butch continues his climb, he mutters, "Don't they get tired? Don't they get hungry? Why don't they slow up? Hell, they could even go faster . . . at least that would be a change!" Butch glances back again, and continues, "They don't even break formation . . . do something!" at which point Butch moves out of the shot, leaving the camera to come to rest on the posse members far off in the distance, in full gallop toward the camera.

A couple of short shots of Butch, Sundance, and the horse continuing to scramble up the mountainside act as a transition to the next scene, which opens with the three of them coming to a stop for a rest on the side of the mountain. As they rest, Butch and Sundance have the following exchange:

Butch: "Kid . . ."

Sundance: "What?"

Butch: "Who's the best lawman?"

Sundance: "'Best'? How? Do you mean toughest . . . or easiest to bribe?"

Butch: "Toughest."

Sundance: "Joe Lefors."

Butch (throwing his head back): "Gotta be."

Sundance: "Lefors never leaves Wyoming . . . *never*. You know that."

Butch: "He always wears a white skipper; that's how you tell it's Joe Lefors, because he wears a white straw hat."

The camera here cuts to the posse members at a full gallop, still far in the distance, but close enough to discern the lead rider is wearing a white hat. The camera returns to a shot of Sundance gazing in the direction of the posse, interrupted just briefly with another shot of the posse. As they get up to continue their ascent of the mountain, Sundance mutters, "Jesus, who are those guys?"

The next scene begins with shots from various angles of Butch and Sundance trying to coax their horse up a steeper grade, but then, the camera abruptly cuts to a distance shot of a large clearing down below the steeper grade, just as the posse members crest a hill at the far end to come into view, and the focus remains on them for nearly ten seconds as they gallop across the clearing, gaining more ground on the struggling Butch and Sundance. The camera then zooms all the way in from this distance shot until it is framing what is in the foreground, mere feet away: Butch, Sundance, and the horse. As the camera follows their progress, it pans upward just enough over Sundance's shoulder to catch the posse continuing their progress across the clearing. The camera then gives a close-up of Sundance looking back over his shoulder, and then cuts to another distance shot of the posse galloping across the clearing.

Butch and Sundance ditch the horse as they approach a rocky portion of the mountain, and the camera follows them as they make their way over and around the boulders making up the face of the mountain. As they are nearing the top, the camera cuts to a high-angle shot down on Butch and Sundance as they stop and look back down, just as the posse members ride into view, a mere thirty feet below them. There is then a cut to a shot across the flattened top of the mountain, with Butch and Sundance emerging into sight over the far edge. They stagger across the top, looking in all directions, and then continue over to the opposite edge, at which point the camera cuts to a low-angle shot capturing them coming over the edge, and sliding down a gravel slope. At the bottom of the slope, the gravel gives way to rock again, and the camera provides a medium shot of Butch and Sundance as they proceed along a rocky plateau, but then pulls back to a position fifty yards away to reveal they are trapped on a rock ledge with a sheer drop-off to a river a hundred feet below.

"How are they possibly going to escape?" That is clearly the reaction to which the audience has been led through the crafting of this segment of the movie. Despite the fact Butch and Sundance are outlaws—the "bad guys"—and those who have managed to corner them are law enforcement officers—the "good guys"—the audience is pulling for Butch and Sundance to prevail. Why? The answer is, "point of view." This entire segment has employed a variety of point-of-view moves designed to have the audience experience all these events through the point of view of Butch and Sundance. These moves establish them as point-of-view characters resulting in the audience feeling empathy for them, thus wishing for a miraculous escape here.

What exactly are the point-of-view moves employed in this segment? It would be wise to reserve a discussion of these moves until after an enumeration of the full range of point-of-view techniques has been provided, and just such an enumeration will be the focus of the next several chapters. Point-of-view dynamics can be conceptualized as operating on six distinct planes,[19] and the particular point-of-view techniques related to each of these planes will be covered in chapters 2–7. Further, discussions of these techniques will be supplemented wherever possible with detailed descriptions of movie scenes employing these techniques, to illustrate what each technique looks like when used in cinematic storytelling—a *moving* picture being worth a thousand words. Then, following a chapter exploring the interaction of point-of-view dynamics on the various planes, chapter 9 will revisit this clip from *Butch Cassidy and the Sundance Kid*, this time flagging the specific point-of-view moves utilized in the crafting of these scenes, moves designed specifically to impact the viewers in such a way as to have them empathizing with Butch and Sundance. After this examination of point of view operating in cinematic storytelling, chapters 10–11 will examine point of view operating in *biblical* storytelling, with a narrative text from each of the testaments being subjected to a full perspective-critical analysis. It is hoped that this combination of descriptive and demonstrative treatments of point of view will provide the biblical interpreter with sufficient equipping to be able to access this deeper level of evaluative guidance present in the point-of-view crafting of biblical narratives.

---

19. Five of these planes are derived from the point-of-view typology of Uspensky, *Poetics*, 8–100; the sixth is derived from Sternberg, *Poetics*, 129–52.

two

Spatial Plane of Point of View

IN CHAPTER 1 OF this work, the concept of point of view was illustrated by means of a picture of an audience being navigated through the world of a story by a tour guide, being held at a distance from some characters and being brought into proximity to others. This reflects dynamics on the *spatial* plane of point of view, and it was offered first because this idea of being given a spatial vantage point from which to experience the elements of the story world is the most accessible entry point into the complex world of point-of-view dynamics.

This is most obvious with cinematic storytelling. At any given point in a film, the viewers are watching the action from some spatial location in the story world, the positioning of the camera taking the shot placing them in that spot. Consider a series of shots from the World War I classic *Lawrence of Arabia* (1962), shots related to an attack on the strategic port of Aqaba. Lawrence, noting Aqaba is only heavily fortified against attack from the sea—since a land attack would require crossing desert considered by all to be impenetrable—leads a team of fifty across the desert to attack the port's vulnerable side.

The first of the series of shots depicts the members of the team as little more than specks stretching across the screen, since the shot is taken from a great distance away;[1] here, the viewers are positioned in the middle of the desert, perhaps one-half mile away from the path of the team. The next shot shows a portion of the team in some detail with a shot taken from considerably closer;[2] the viewers are still positioned in the middle of the

1. At 1:02:23—1:03:00.
2. At 1:03:01—1:03:19.

desert, but now in a location only ten yards away from the path of the riders. After this comes a shot focusing on a single rider, this shot being taken from right up close to this character;[3] the viewers are now positioned just a few yards away. Therefore, in this one-minute sequence, the viewers have been situated in three different locations in the desert, and this has been accomplished simply through changes in camera positioning.

Of course, with written narrative, the spatial positioning of the readers is not as obvious. Still, something akin to the positioning of cameras does occur with written narratives. As mentioned in chapter 1, as readers proceed through a narrative, they have images form *in their mind's eye*, and these images will necessarily have a spatial aspect to them. What is being viewed will be in some spatial relation to the readers, whether that be close up, or at a distance. However, the spatial positioning of the readers is not accomplished through the movement of cameras, but rather, through the use of certain literary techniques designed to create the illusion of close-up shots or distance shots in the readers' mind's eye.

The key distinction in the analysis of the spatial plane is whether the narrator is drawing the readers into a position in proximity to a particular character, or pulling the readers back into a position at a distance from the character. With this in mind, we shall now embark on an examination of the variety of options available to narrators as they map out the spatial plane of a narrative.

Following a Single Character

A prominent spatial-plane technique utilized in all genres of storytelling involves having the audience become "joined at the hip" with a particular character, such that the audience is made to follow the character wherever he or she goes. With this strategy, the audience is kept in proximity to this one character and, as a result, is positioned to encounter all the same situations encountered by the character, and experience them in the same way the character experiences them. This leads the audience to view these situations in the same way the character views them, in other words, through the character's point of view.

Usually, a constant positioning of an audience in proximity to a particular character is innocuous enough that the audience will not even

---

3. At 1:03:20—1:03:26.

Perspective Criticism

notice it is happening. Even so, the audience will still be influenced by it. A striking cinematic example of this technique is found in *Das Boot* (1985), a film about the crew of a German submarine during the Second World War. At the sixteen-minute mark of the movie, the submarine heads out to sea, and the cameras stay exclusively on its crew for over three hours, until it reaches its ultimate destination a mere five minutes from the end of the film.[4] This long stretch of the movie consists almost entirely of shots inside—and very occasionally outside—the submarine, thus constituting a rather unique experience of following not just a single character, but the crew as a collective character.[5]

It should be noted there is nothing inherent in the storyline of this film that necessitates it being shot in this way. Typically, a movie of this sort would consist mainly of shots in and around the sub, but would also have some shots back at the home base, and some ahead at the destination, and perhaps even some on enemy vessels. However, each shot of this sort would interrupt the following of the crew, and thus, break the spell being cast on the viewers. The total absence of any such interruptions in *Das Boot* means the spell is able to continue for hours, contributing toward the viewers developing a strong feeling of empathy for these German sailors.

As mentioned, this type of following of a collective character is rather unique. When the spatial-plane technique of following is employed, it is almost always with a particular character. An example of this is seen in *Apocalypse Now* (1979), a story set in the Vietnam War focusing on a Captain Willard of the U.S. military who is sent on a clandestine mission to eliminate a highly decorated American colonel who is believed to have gone insane.

The storyline begins with scenes in Willard's room in Saigon,[6] and as he moves, the camera moves along with him: first, to the Nha Trang airfield;[7] then, on his trip to a rendezvous point where he is to pick up an escort to the mouth of the Nung River;[8] then, during his time at the

---

4. The time references all relate to the director's cut of the movie.

5. The submarine does dock in a port at one point, during which time the camera does leave the sub for a seven-minute stretch as some of the crew members go to meet with superior officers (side 2, 33:36—40:20), but even here, the camera continues to follow a sub-group of the collective character.

6. Disc 1, 1:42—9:21 (all time signatures are to the original 1979 version of the movie).

7. Disc 1, 9:22—18:53.

8. Disc 1, 18:54—27:11.

rendezvous point;[9] then, in his participation in an attack on a village at the mouth of the Nung River;[10] then, as he navigates his way up the river to the colonel's compound;[11] then, during his time at the compound, where the rest of the storyline plays itself out.[12] Willard himself appears in the vast majority of the shots making up the movie, and when he is not actually present in a shot, he is still in the vicinity of the camera, meaning even these shots are capturing the locale being experienced by Willard. Through this following of Willard by the camera, the viewers are kept constantly in a position close to him, and thus, right in the middle of whatever is happening to him. As a result, the viewers end up experiencing all the same events Willard experiences, and this contributes toward a merging of the viewers with this character.

The most obvious biblical example of this dynamic of following a particular character is the treatment of Jesus in each of the gospels, where the readers are kept in proximity to Jesus practically anywhere he goes, as opposed to having them follow other characters. For example, Mark's account of Jesus' ministry—from launch to arrest (1:9—14:50)—consists of 587 verses, and in 95 percent of these verses, the readers are positioned in the vicinity of Jesus, the only pericope taking the readers away from Jesus for any significant stretch of the narrative being the account of the death of John the Baptist (6:14–29). Clearly, the Marcan narrator is having the readers follow Jesus, a strategy that contributes toward the establishing of Jesus as a point-of-view character.

The case of Jesus in the gospels is exceptional; nowhere else in the Bible is there another example of a narrator having the readers follow a character for anywhere near this extent. However, this spatial-plane technique used for shorter stretches can be found in many places in the narratives of the Bible.

Consider, for example, the case of Naaman and Elisha in 2 Kgs 5:1–19a, imagining the events of this passage being filmed, and keeping track of the spatial location of the movie camera throughout. The first verse sets the context by explaining that Naaman is a highly regarded commander of the army of the king of Aram, and that he has leprosy. In verses 2–3, Naaman discovers from his wife there is a prophet in Samaria who could

---

9. Disc 1, 27:12—35:37.
10. Disc 1, 35:38—50:12.
11. Disc 1, 50:13—disc 2, 23:41.
12. Disc 2, 23:42—1:06:03.

heal him; here, the camera is situated in the house of Naaman. Verses 4–5a establish a new spatial location, the palace of the king of Aram, where Naaman receives permission to seek out the healing, and obtains a letter to be delivered to the king of Israel; so, as Naaman moves from his home to the palace, the camera follows him. Verses 5b–7 establish yet another new spatial location, the palace of the king of Israel. Here, Naaman is shown travelling there and delivering the letter; here, again, the camera follows Naaman as he moves to the new location.

Verse 8 reads, "When Elisha . . . heard that the king had torn his robes, he sent word to the king, saying, 'Why have you torn your robes? Let him come to me . . .'" The fact Elisha is portrayed as hearing the news of the king and sending his response indicates he is situated in a location other than the king's palace. Further, Naaman is clearly not present in this other location with Elisha, thus suggesting the camera has ceased following Naaman by moving on to this other location without him. This, however, is not the case. While this verse does imply Elisha is situated in some other location, it does not actually establish this place as a new location in the story, as would a statement such as, "Now, Elisha was in his house . . ." Rather, the actions of Elisha reported in this verse are depicted as occurring in a spatial vacuum, and since verse 8 does not involve a new spatial location, the camera would still be back at the palace—where Naaman is situated—and thus, would still be following him.

Verses 9–10 describe Naaman coming to the entrance of Elisha's house where he receives instructions from Elisha to wash seven times in the Jordan in order to be cleansed; here, a new spatial location is established, and the camera is there with Naaman. In verses 11–13, Naaman storms off in indignation because Elisha's instructions do not meet his expectations, and his servants go after him to convince him to heed the instructions. Another spatial location is established—some point up the road from Elisha's house—and the camera again follows Naaman to this point. Verse 14 establishes another spatial location at the Jordan River, and the camera follows Naaman there to show him dipping himself seven times and being cleansed. Verses 15–19a describe Naaman's return to Elisha's house and a final exchange between the two men, with the camera following Naaman from the Jordan to Elisha's house.

In this passage, every time Naaman moves from one spatial location to another, the camera moves with him. As a result, the camera is always situated in proximity to this character. This, in turn, keeps the readers situated in proximity to Naaman, a dynamic that contributes toward them coming to merge with this character.

Linguistics Affecting Readers' Distance from Characters

As established at the outset of this chapter, analysis of point of view on the spatial plane is all about whether the readers of a narrative text are being positioned in proximity to, or at a distance from, a given character. Linguist Susumu Kuno offers some innovative insights into how various linguistic constructions naturally produce senses of proximity or distance. His discussions do not actually speak in terms of the literary concept of point of view. Rather, he speaks in terms of "empathy," which he conceptualizes as involving various camera angles produced by syntactic constructions: "In producing natural sentences, speakers unconsciously make the same kind of decisions that film directors make about where to place themselves with respect to the events and states that their sentences are intended to describe."[13] This description, of course, reflects the definition of point of view developed in chapter 1 of the present work, and so, Kuno's analysis of syntactic constructions should prove helpful for our purposes.

According to Kuno, certain syntactic constructions in a statement reflect that the speaker of the statement feels a greater sense of identification, or empathy, with one of the persons mentioned in the statement than another. Kuno formalizes his discussion of these various syntactic constructions by means of a series of empathy hierarchies, each indicating to which person mentioned in a statement the speaker feels more empathy. All of this relates quite readily to the analysis of biblical narratives by thinking in terms of a "narrator" (as opposed to a "speaker") feeling more empathy—and encouraging the readers to feel more empathy—for one "character" over against another (as opposed to one "person" over against another).

A number of the empathy hierarchies developed by Kuno can be subsumed under what he calls the *Syntactic Prominence Principle*, which reads,

---

13. Kuno, *Functional Syntax*. Kuno's basic interest is in how different syntactic constructions in a clause may be conflicting in terms of the empathy impulses they are sending to the reader, thus making them grammatically unacceptable. This, of course, is not our concern. However, Kuno's discussions on the empathy impulses created by various syntactic constructions can provide us with valuable guidelines for our examination of how point-of-view crafting impacts empathy dynamics in biblical narratives.

Perspective Criticism

"Give syntactic prominence to a person/object that you are empathizing with."[14] Again, Kuno's concern is with the acceptability of grammatical constructions, and he provides this principle as a guide toward that end. However, it is simple to reword this principle to make it relevant to biblical interpreters trying to determine with which character in a narrative the readers are being led to empathize; for interpreters analyzing a narrative passage, "the readers are being led to empathize with the character that is being given syntactic prominence," with "syntactic prominence" understood as being placed close to the head of a clause.

Though Kuno does not provide a detailed explanation of his thinking behind the idea of syntactic prominence producing empathy, some reflection on the way in which the viewers of a movie are impacted by the unfolding nature of a storyline makes this clear. In opening a new scene, the director has many options in terms of how the viewers are going to meet the characters involved in the scene. To name a few, the director may start with a setting bereft of characters, and then have a character enter to fill the void, followed by the entry of other characters; or the director may open the scene with one character present, and subsequently have other characters join him or her; or the director may start the scene with the camera focused on a single character, but then have the camera pull back and pan to one side to reveal the presence of other characters.

Though these various options may appear at first glance to be quite distinct from each other, they all have one thing in common: each involves the viewers being draw to one particular character before encountering any of the other characters. And when this happens, the viewers will be inclined to perceive the secondary characters through the perspective of the primary character.

In cinematic storytelling, this dynamic is subtle; therefore, when it occurs, it will usually not even be noticed by the viewers. However, a scene from the movie *Thelma and Louise* (1991) presents this dynamic in a rather dramatic fashion. In this film, the title characters are best friends who decide to go on a weekend fishing trip. However, while on the way, Thelma almost gets raped in a parking lot, being saved by Louise arriving with a gun. And while they are leaving, Louise ends up shooting the would-be rapist dead. They are able to avoid detection for a long time, but the police do finally catch up to them, resulting in a wild car chase, and it

---

14. Kuno, *Functional Syntax*, 232.

is in the context of this chase that the scene in question takes place.[15] The camera catches the women's car with a high-angle shot trailing the car as it races across a barren wasteland away from the camera. The camera gradually falls back, allowing the car to pull away, but as it does, a police vehicle enters the bottom of the screen in hot pursuit . . . and then another . . . and then another, until eleven are shown fanned out behind the women's car.

The appearance of just the women's car at the beginning of the shot establishes an initial focal point for the viewers. And with this focal point established, each of the other vehicles entering the shot are perceived in light of the initial car. To put it another way, the viewers are led to consider the police vehicles through the point of view of the women in the initial car.

The account of a young Saul and a servant searching for some lost donkeys (1 Sam 9:3–14) demonstrates what this dynamic looks like in a biblical narrative. After much searching, Saul is ready to give up, but the servant suggests they consult a man of God in a nearby town. When approaching the town, they find out from some girls he has just arrived to bless sacrifices the townspeople are making that day. Then verse 14 reports, "And they went up to the town. They came to the middle of the town, and behold! Samuel was coming out toward them, going out to the high place."

To this point, the readers have been led to follow the exploits of Saul and the servant for eleven straight verses. Therefore, when Samuel appears on the scene in verse 14, the readers cannot help but perceive him in light of their preceding experience of Saul and the servant. That being the case, the spatial location of a camera filming the appearance of Samuel would be in proximity to Saul and the servant, shooting away from them toward Samuel.

As mentioned earlier, Kuno has developed a number of empathy hierarchies, each covering a different linguistic construction. Most of them are not relevant for our purposes, and we will restrict our look at his work to only two of them. The first is his *Surface Structure Empathy Hierarchy*, which reads, "It is easier for the speaker to empathize with the referent of the subject than with the referent of other [noun phrases] in the sentence."[16] It is clear how this hierarchy is subsumed under the Syntactic Prominence Principle cited above—according to which empathy resides in the person/object that is closest to the head of a clause—for English word usage

---

15. At 1:58:19—1:58:27.
16. Kuno, *Functional Syntax*, 211.

generally follows the pattern of "subject / verb / object" ("S-V-O"), thus placing the subject in the position of syntactic prominence.

Of course, word-order conventions in biblical Hebrew and Greek are not nearly as fixed as those of English, and the conventions that do appear most regularly do not follow the S-V-O pattern of English, but rather, prefer to have the verb at the head of a clause. However, although the subject is not typically found at the head of a clause, it is typically the first noun phrase encountered. This means that of all the characters mentioned in a clause, it will be the referent of the subject that is most often in the position of syntactic prominence, and thus, the character most often engendering the empathy of the readers. Therefore, despite the fact word-order conventions in biblical Hebrew and Greek do not follows those of English, Kuno's Surface Structure Empathy Hierarchy should still be relevant for the analysis of empathy dynamics in biblical narratives.

It should be noted, however, that while what Kuno says may work well at the level of the single statement, it works less well when analyzing a whole narrative passage, for among the various clauses making up a passage, the subject can change frequently, sometimes as frequently as every clause. Therefore, an attempt to discern empathy dynamics simply through noting which character is acting as subject will usually prove unfruitful. Still, Kuno's Surface Structure Empathy Hierarchy can have relevance in the discerning of empathy dynamics if used on a more narrow basis.

As mentioned, in both biblical Hebrew and Greek, there exists a strong tendency to front the subject of every clause, that is, to have it appear as the first noun phrase of the clause. Therefore, a closer look is warranted in situations where the subject is not the first noun phrase in a clause—having been supplanted by some non-subject noun phrase—for this non-typical construction may have been selected with a mind toward giving the non-subject noun phrase syntactic prominence in an attempt to have the readers empathize with its referent.

In isolating clauses of this type for consideration, it is important to exclude cases where a non-subject *pronoun* supplants a subject as the first noun-phrase of a clause, as happens in Matt 21:14 in the introduction to a confrontation between Jesus and some Jewish religious leaders: *kai prosēlthon autō tuphloi kai chōloi en tō hierō* ("And approached him blind ones and lame ones in the temple.") The dative *autō*, whose antecedent is Jesus, does precede the compound subject "blind ones and lame ones." However, placing a non-subject pronoun immediately following the verb

Spatial Plane of Point of View

like this is very common, and even a cursory look at the functioning of such pronouns in biblical narratives reveals they play no significant role with regards to empathy dynamics. Only in cases where a non-subject *noun* has been fronted to a position preceding the subject is there significance in this regard.

Consider, for example, Matt 15:1. This introduction to an earlier confrontation between Jesus and some Jewish religious leaders reads: *tote proserchontai tō Iēsou apo Ierosolymōn Pharisaioi kai grammateis* ("Then approaches Jesus from Jerusalem Pharisees and scribes"). Here, it is the dative proper noun "Jesus" that has been fronted to a position preceding the compound subject "Pharisees and scribes." Further, this type of construction appears so infrequently that any occurrence of it stands out. In this case, the character Jesus is afforded syntactic prominence over against the Pharisees and scribes, and this inclines the readers to perceive these Jewish religious leaders through the point of view of Jesus.

Another of Kuno's empathy hierarchies, the *Word Order Empathy Hierarchy*, is also subsumed under his Syntactic Prominence Principle. It reads, "It is easier for the speaker to empathize with the referent of a left-hand [noun phrase] in a coordinate structure than with that of a right-hand [noun phrase]";[17] again, because the left-hand noun phrase is closer to the head of the clause, it would be more syntactically prominent than the right-hand noun phrase.

For an instance where this hierarchy comes into play in a biblical narrative, consider coordinate structures involving Saul and Barnabas in the book of Acts. These two characters are mentioned together for the first time in an account of relief being sent by the Antioch church to the Jerusalem church (11:27–30); this passage ends with a mention that the relief is sent by the hand of "Barnabas and Saul" (v. 30). Then, following the report of Peter's miraculous delivery from prison, the focus returns briefly to the two as they complete their task, and they are again cited as "Barnabas and Saul" (12:25). Then, once the two leave on a missionary journey, the account of their stay in Paphos on Cyprus includes mention that proconsul Sergius Paulus summons "Barnabas and Saul" (13:7). Therefore, the first three times the narrator refers to these two characters using a coordinate structure, he mentions Barnabas first, and then Saul.[18] As a result, the read-

---

17. Kuno, *Functional Syntax*, 232.

18. There is an additional occurrence of "Barnabas and Saul" in this stretch of text as well. In the account of them being commissioned for their journey, the Holy Spirit is

ers come to sense themselves in a spatial position closer to Barnabas than to Saul, and thus, are more inclined to empathize with Barnabas than with Saul during this stretch of text.

This conclusion may seem counter-intuitive, given the prominence of Saul/Paul in the storyline of Acts. However, that prominence is largely attributable to how he is portrayed subsequent to this stretch of text. To this point in the storyline, coverage of his ministry activity has consisted of only two short accounts of preaching attempts, neither of which includes any indication of success (9:20–25, 28–29); other than that, he is simply shown doing what Barnabas is doing. Barnabas, on the other hand, has been shown giving sacrificially in the face of need in the Jerusalem church (4:36–37), interceding for Saul with disciples in Jerusalem who are afraid of him (9:26–27), being entrusted with the task of checking out the great number of Gentiles who are joining the church in Antioch (11:22), and being the one to fetch Saul from his training in Tarsus to begin his ministry (11:25–26). At the time the two of them embark on their journey at the beginning of chapter 13, Barnabas is firmly established in the ministry of the church, whereas Saul has barely begun to contribute. This being the case, it is not surprising the Lukan narrator would manipulate point of view on the spatial plane by means of the order of names in the coordinate structures in 11:30, 12:25, and 13:7, in order to have the readers positioned closer to Barnabas than to Saul.

Degree of Detail

As we have seen, when moviegoers are watching a particular scene of a film, their vantage point is fixed for them by the positioning of the camera taking the shot. Further, moviegoers are not apt to address their minds to the issue of their spatial positioning in the story world of the movie. Rather, they simply allow themselves to be placed here and there in the spatial dimension of the story world without any awareness of the fact the positioning of the camera is responsible for their spatial positions.

Occasionally, this spell of unawareness will be broken by camera work that puts spatial positioning at issue. We saw one example of this in our look at *Lawrence of Arabia* earlier in this chapter. Recall how the excursion

---

depicted as saying, "Set apart for me *Barnabas and Saul . . .*" (13:2). However, this coordinate structure occurs in the direct discourse of a character in the story, whereas it is only coordinate structures in narratorial speech that are to be considered.

across the desert includes a shot where the camera is drawn far back, to the point where the men on camels are little more than specks on the screen, with absolutely no detail about them being provided to the viewers. This type of camera work is so extreme it causes the viewers to take note of the fact they are being spatially positioned—specifically, the fact they are being positioned a great distance from the characters making this excursion—done for the purpose of having them fully appreciate the vast expanse of nothingness involved in this venture.

Spatial positioning can also be brought to the viewers' attention in the opposite direction, that is, with the viewers being drawn in close to some detail of significance in the story world. Consider, for example, a scene from *Citizen Kane* (1941), a film about an eccentric publishing tycoon. The movie begins with Kane uttering the enigmatic name "Rosebud" just as he dies, and the rest of the film consists of an investigation to determine the significance of "Rosebud," though the investigators end up conceding defeat. The closing sequence of the movie captures the beginning of the process of disposing of all Kane's earthly possessions that have been gathered in a warehouse-sized room.[19] The camera starts with a high-angle shot to show the enormous breadth of the room, then slowly pans across the thousands of items, gradually zooming in on one portion of the room, and then in further on an old wooden sled. The camera reaches a position about ten feet away—from which some stenciled lettering is apparent on the top of the sled—just as a worker picks it up and carries it off.

The camera then cuts to a huge furnace in the room, just as the worker approaches it and throws in the sled. The camera draws in on the furnace until it captures the sled in the fire from a position about five feet away, shooting through the door of the furnace; with this shot, a single word stenciled across the top of the sled is clearly visible: "Rosebud." The camera cuts to a position a mere eighteen inches from the sled, focusing in on the word "Rosebud," and then very slowly zooms in on it until the camera is so close that "Rosebud" almost fills the screen.

The distance estimates just given are based upon seeing the sled on the screen and estimating how far from the camera it is situated at any given moment. With a depiction of an object in a written narrative, on the other hand, the readers do not have the benefit of seeing the object on a screen to estimate how far from the object they are situated. However, the *degree*

---

19. At 1:54:41—1:56:17.

of detail in written depictions of objects provides readers with help in this regard.

Consider the above written depictions of the sled. The first mentions that "some stenciled lettering" is apparent on the sled, representing a moderate degree of detail; it is a higher degree of detail than merely saying there is "something" stenciled on the sled, but a lower degree of detail than providing what is actually spelled by the lettering. Note further that recognizing this degree of detail allows for an estimate of how far the readers are being situated from the sled. On the one hand, being close enough to see the stenciling consists of actual letters, and not just shapes, indicates a distance of no more than fifteen feet. On the other hand, not being close enough to make out what the lettering spells reflects a distance of no less than ten feet. Therefore, the inclusion in the depiction of the sled that there is "some stenciled lettering" on it indicates the readers are situated between ten to fifteen feet away from it.

The second depiction of the sled mentions capturing the sled "in the fire . . . shooting through the door of the furnace . . . a single word stenciled across the top of the sled is clearly visible: 'Rosebud.'" The detail that the word "Rosebud" is clearly visible indicates the sled is no more than seven feet away. However, the detail the shot is taken from a position outside the furnace indicates a distance of no less than four feet. Again, a reasonably precise distance estimate can be established simply by attending to the details of the description of the sled.

Though biblical narratives are generally sparse when it comes to details, there are enough provided to warrant considering whether a degree-of-detail analysis of a narrative passage might aid in establishing how far from a given person or object the readers are being positioned. Consider, for example, the account of Saul's Damascus Road experience (Acts 9:1–9). This passage depicts Saul as falling to the ground upon experiencing a light from heaven shining around him, and encountering the risen Jesus. In verse 8, the Lukan narrator makes mention of two separate details: Saul's getting up from the ground, and his opening his eyes. The inclusion of the first detail produces in the readers' mind's eye the image of a man first lying on the ground, and then rising to his feet. Unfortunately, this detail is not helpful in establishing how far from Saul the readers are being positioned, for this is a detail that could be perceived by the readers whether they are positioned three-hundred feet from Saul, or just three feet from him. However, analysis of the second detail narrows the range considerably. This detail produces in the readers' mind's eye the image of a pair of eyes closed, but then, the eye lids opening. This is something that definitely could not be seen from three-hundred feet away. Rather, to see this movement of Saul's eye lids would require the readers to be up close to Saul. Therefore, the inclusion of this detail constitutes evidence the narrator is here positioning the readers in proximity to Saul.

Establishing Sense of Distance From Characters

The discussion to this point has focused on ways in which a narrator can provide the readers with a sense of proximity to a character for the purpose of establishing that character as a point-of-view character. However, not every narrative passage is going to have a point-of-view character, as the narrator may wish for the readers to remain detached from all the characters in the passage, and this necessitates that the narrator create a sense of distance between the readers and all the characters. This section lays out some techniques used to create such a sense.

Sequential Survey

Uspensky uses the term "sequential survey" to designate a scene where a narrator moves the readers sequentially from one character to another and to another as a means of preventing the readers from establishing a position in proximity to any particular character.[20] A film utilizing this technique for practically the whole of its story is *Twelve Angry Men* (1957). This is a movie focusing on the deliberations of the jury in a murder trial, and apart from a brief introduction and an equally brief conclusion, the whole of the action occurs within the confines of a jury deliberation room.[21]

The bulk of the action in the deliberation room is simply filmed with the camera moving around the room to capture each contribution to the deliberations as it is given. The result is a sequential survey of all the members of the jury. This style of filming means, of course, the camera tends to alight on any particular character only briefly, before moving on to another.

---

20. Uspensky, *Poetics*, 60–62.
21. For a short segment of the movie, the action does spill over into an accompanying washroom, but this is not material for our purposes.

Perspective Criticism

As a result, the viewers are not allowed to become settled at the side of any one of them.

A biblical example of a sequential survey is found in the report of the proceedings of the Jerusalem Council (Acts 15:1–21). The account of the proceedings begins with a summary statement indicating there was much debate (v. 7a). Then the camera focuses in on Peter to capture a short speech he makes (vv. 7b–11). Then the camera cuts to Barnabas and Paul as they provide testimony of what they have witnessed while ministering among the Gentiles (v. 12). Then the camera cuts to James for the rendering of the decision (vv. 13–21). This hopping from character to character prevents the readers from establishing a position in proximity to any one of them and, as a result, none of them come to be seen as the point-of-view character of this passage.

Bird's-Eye View

Like the sequential survey, a bird's-eye view covers a number of characters. However, unlike the sequential survey, it does not cover them one at a time, but rather, uses a wide-angle shot of all the characters at one time. An example of this from the world of film is found in *Seven Samurai* (1954), the story of a village of peasants who hire a group of unemployed Samurai warriors to protect the village. The movie begins with a group of bandits deciding to raid the village, but postponing the raid until after the barley harvest is in. Then comes a short shot taken from a high angle down on the village, showing dozens of figures hunched down on the ground in a tight circle in the middle of the village.[22] Because of their distance from the camera—perhaps seventy yards away—no one figure is distinguishable from any other. Rather, this bird's-eye shot is designed to capture the village—and its inhabitants—as a whole, and in so doing, create a sense of distance from any particular villager.

In this example from the world of film, the camera shot is actually taken from the vantage point of the birds, that is, from high up. A biblical passage that exhibits this type of vantage point is Num 11:31 and its depiction of God providing quail for the people of Israel in response to their hankering after having meat to eat. This verse relates how the Lord causes quail to be blown into the Israelites' camp, with the description of this event including the detail that the quantity of quail was such that they

22. At 4:48—4:52.

cover an area one day's journey in every direction to a depth of two cubits. Visualizing the image created by this description requires being high up over the camp, high enough to be able to see at one time the whole of an area encompassing a day's journey in every direction. And, of course, being positioned that high up creates within the readers a distinct sense of distance from any particular person going about gathering the quail.

Silent Scene

A technique used less frequently than the preceding two is what Uspensky calls a "silent scene."[23] This involves a positioning at a distance from the characters involved in a scene, but not necessarily at as great a distance as that involved with a bird's eye view. Rather, the positioning is close enough that the audience is able to observe what the characters are doing, but the audience is not close enough to be able to hear what the characters are saying. Therefore, a silent scene is characterized by description in some detail of characters interacting with each other but, at the same time, an absence of any indication of what the characters are saying.

For a filmic example of this technique, consider a brief scene from *Titanic* (1997), a love story set aboard the Titanic involving a working-class boy and an aristocratic girl already engaged to be married to another man. The scene occurs following a formal dinner, where the men of the party, including the girl's fiancé, withdraw to the smoking room for brandy and discussion of business and politics. It depicts four men sitting around a table with their brandy and cigarettes, and engaging in a discussion,[24] though the content of their conversation cannot be discerned, despite the fact the viewers are positioned no more than a few feet away. A scene that ordinarily would include the content of these discussions has essentially been converted into a silent scene, and this functions to distance the viewers from these characters.

The narratives of the Bible use a device akin to a silent scene, a device characterized by the same features exhibited in this scene from *Titanic*. Consider, for example, the introduction to an account in Mark in which Jesus is shown casting an evil spirit out of a boy (Mark 9:14). It reads, "And coming toward the disciples, [Jesus, Peter, James, and John] saw a large crowd around them and scribes contending with them." This verse depicts

23. Uspensky, *Poetics*, 65.
24. At 1:08:25—1:08:32 of disc 1.

quite a commotion, suggesting shouting back and forth. However, despite the fact this occurrence is verbal in nature, the verse contains no indication of any of the words being exchanged. We have here a silent scene in that it deprives the readers of the content of the confrontation. As a result, the readers are distanced from the participants in this melee.

Conclusion

When analyzing what point-of-view moves are occurring on the spatial plane of a narrative text, the factor outweighing all others by a wide margin is whether or not the narrator is leading the readers to follow a given character. This technique constitutes a powerful tool for establishing and maintaining readers in a position in proximity to a given character. However, it must be recognized that a following of a character, even for a substantial segment of a narrative, will not necessarily establish that character as a point-of-view character.[25]

In situations where the following of a particular character is not a prominent factor, ascertaining the distance the readers are being placed from the various characters of a scene should prove helpful in determining whether or not a point-of-view character is being established for the scene. And consideration of the degree of detail present in the depiction of the scene, and of which characters are being afforded syntactic prominence, may be valuable in making that determination.

---

25. See the section entitled "Proximity on Spatial Plane / Distance on Psychological Plane" in chapter 8 for a discussion of a particular type of following that does not create within the readers a sense of proximity to the character being followed.

three

Psychological Plane of Point of View

THE PRECEDING CHAPTER DEMONSTRATED how the way in which an audience is spatially positioned within a story world can make a significant contribution toward whether the audience experiences a given character as a point-of-view character, thus tending to evaluate his or her actions positively. The current chapter explores what might be considered a special case of spatial positioning, that is, the situation where the audience is placed repeatedly inside the head of a character versus the situation where the audience is kept entirely outside of the character. We will follow Uspensky's lead in considering these dynamics as pertaining to an entirely separate plane, what he calls the *psychological* plane.

INSIDE VIEWS

Central to the manipulation of point of view on the psychological plane are *inside views*—that is, glimpses into the inner workings of a character. Practically all analysis of the psychological plane consists simply of distinguishing between instances when the readers are treated to a *subjective* experience of a character by virtue of inside views, and when they are relegated to the status of mere *objective* bystanders, able to observe only the exterior of the character.

It is not difficult to see how inside views could make a contribution toward the establishing of a character as a point-of-view character. When the readers experience the elements of the story world from a vantage point inside a character—thinking along with the character's thoughts, feeling the emotions being felt by the character—their perspective on the story world is coordinated with that of the character. To put it another way, the readers are experiencing the story world as filtered through the character's psychological point of view.

An exceptionally vivid illustration of this dynamic from the world of film is seen in *A Beautiful Mind* (2001), the account of the career of mathematician John Nash. The story opens as Nash begins his first year in a doctoral program in mathematics at Princeton University. In an early scene,[1] Nash is just settling into his dorm room when he hears someone at his door. When he looks in that direction, he sees a young man stagger into the room, announcing he is Nash's roommate. Nash simply looks at him, and mumbles, ". . . roommate?" But before he can say anything more, the young man is in the room, turning off Nash's music, then stripping off his own shoes, jacket, and shirt, all the while pontificating on hangovers. Finally, he walks over to Nash, extends his hand, and says, "John Nash?" And after Nash responds with a weak "Hello," the young man continues with, "Charles Herman . . . pleased to meet you," before walking away, leaving Nash totally nonplussed.

At first glance, this scene appears to be unremarkable, with little value in a discussion of inside views. However, what will be revealed later in the movie is the fact that Nash never had a roommate, enjoying a dorm room to himself his whole time at Princeton, and Charles was merely a delusion of Nash resulting from an undiagnosed case of schizophrenia. This means, of course, Nash is actually alone in his room throughout this scene, and the presence of Charles is only in his mind. Further, the fact the viewers also see Charles means the viewers must be experiencing an *inside view* of Nash; that is, they must be occupying a vantage point inside Nash's mind, the only vantage point from which Charles could be perceived.

The creation of subsequent inside views of Nash requires some especially deft camera work, for Charles must be included in scenes in such a way as to give the impression Nash sees him but, at the same time, not make it obvious no one else is able to do so. By way of contrast, inside views in written narratives are simple to execute, often requiring no more than clauses introduced by *verba sentiendi*, that is, verbs having to do with thinking and feeling. For example, an inside view into what a character happens to be thinking can be brought about simply with "She thought

---

1. At 4:59—6:12.

that . . ." We will encounter *verba sentiendi* in a number of the categories of inside views discussed below.

Expressions of Thinking

The category of narratorial statements indicating what a character is thinking is a good place to start in a discussion of specific types of inside views, for they so clearly display an inner working of a character—something an objective observer would not be able to discern. Because such constructions are so commonplace, it is easy to lose sight of the fact they do actually have the effect of taking readers inside a character. This effect is harder to miss in cinematic storytelling, where the providing of a character's thoughts necessitates artificial devices. One such device is a character *voice-over*, with the character's voice being heard in the soundtrack when the character is not talking, but merely thinking.[2] This type of voice-over can be found throughout *Adaptation* (2002), a film about screenwriter Charlie Kaufman who has been engaged to turn a plotless book into a screenplay. An early scene in the movie captures Charlie as he is just starting his work on the screenplay, and part of this scene employs a character voice-over.[3]

The scene opens with Charlie sitting in front of his typewriter. As he stares ahead in silence, his voice can be heard, saying in a slow, methodical fashion, "To begin . . . to begin . . . how to start . . . I'm hungry . . . I should get coffee . . . coffee would help me think . . . but I should write something first, then reward myself with coffee . . . coffee and a muffin . . . okay, so I need to establish the theme . . . maybe banana-nut . . . that's a good muffin . . ." Without the voice-over, this scene would have consisted simply of a half minute of nothing more than Charlie sitting silently in front of his typewriter, leaving the viewers to wonder what he is thinking. However, the inclusion of the voice-over provides the viewers with a glimpse into Charlie's mind. The viewers are made privy to each thought as it emerges into Charlie's consciousness, each effort to focus on the task at hand, as well as each distraction. Being fed this blow-by-blow account, the viewers

---

2. The dynamic discussed here is to be distinguished from a character voice-over that is not reflecting the thoughts passing through a character's mind, but rather, is providing commentary directed at the viewers, for example, the voice-over of Red in *The Shawshank Redemption* (1994).

3. At 13:49—14:20.

experience the stream of thoughts right along with Charlie, an experience that contributes to the process of having the viewers merge with Charlie.

For the purpose of presenting the thoughts swirling in a film character's mind, this type of voice-over is rarely used, with movie directors more often resorting to what could be called "verbalized expressions of thoughts." These expressions appear simply to be direct discourse, since a character is actually shown speaking. However, on closer examination, it becomes obvious what is being said is not being directed toward another character; in fact, there may not even be another character present. Rather, these expressions are spoken to no one in particular, and would probably not have been spoken at all, except the director wants the viewers to become privy to a character's thoughts at that particular point in the movie.

An example of this is seen near the beginning of *The Godfather* (1972), the story of a New York mafia family during the 1930s. Early in the movie, within the context of a wedding on the family's estate, there is a brief scene of the bride and groom in a receiving line, accepting an envelope from a guest, with the bride putting it into a fancy bag. The camera then cuts to Paulie Gatto—the personal chauffeur to the family's don—as he watches the bride and groom from a distance, and says, "Twenty . . . thirty grand. In small bills . . . cash. In that little silk purse. *Madon'* . . . if this was someone else's wedding . . . *sfortunato* ['bad luck']." Significant for our purposes is the fact Paulie is not saying these words to some other character, for he is standing alone as he speaks them. Rather, Paulie is simply giving verbal expression to what he is thinking at that moment, thus providing the viewers with an inside view of the workings of his mind.

While movie makersmovie makers require artificial devices such as these to convey a character's thoughts to the viewers, biblical narrators are able to accomplish this task with ease. They need only employ one of the *verba sentiendi* to introduce the content of a character's thoughts. The narratives of the Bible are littered with such constructions. One example is found in Mark 6:45–52, which reports the disciples engaged in a journey by boat following Jesus' feeding of the five thousand. Jesus has made them go ahead of him, but hours later, he catches up to them walking on the water, with verse 49 reporting, "When they saw him walking on the sea, they *thought* that it was a ghost." Just as the viewers of *Adaptation* are taken into the mind of Charlie, and the viewers of the *The Godfather* are taken into the mind of Paulie, so also the readers of Mark's gospel are taken into the minds of the disciples with this inside view into what they *think* they are witnessing.

Expressions of Emotions

As with expressions of thinking, narratorial statements indicating what a character is feeling constitute inside views into the character's inner life. In the genre of film, providing inside views into a character's emotions poses a challenge, for a movie camera is limited to the exterior of the character, with no way of taking shots of his or her inner emotional life. Of course, a camera is able to capture a scowl as an indication of an angry inner state, or a smile as evidence of a happy state. However, these facial expressions cannot be trusted as reliable indicators of those states, for a genuine facial expression and a faked one can look identical to the camera. Therefore, a moviegoer has no way of knowing for sure whether a facial expression truly does indicate a particular inner emotional state, or is simply a convincing ruse.

Consider a scene from *Gone With the Wind* (1939), the story of a southern belle named Scarlett O'Hara during the tumultuous years of the American Civil War and its aftermath. The scene occurs at a point in the movie when Scarlett, recovering from almost losing the family plantation, plans to start a lumber business. When she discovers Ashley Wilkes—with whom she is secretly in love—is planning to leave the area, she tells him she was counting on him to help her start the lumber business, and even offers him a half-share in the business. When Ashley refuses to relent, Scarlett is shown collapsing onto a couch, burying her face in her hands and weeping uncontrollably.

At first glance, it would appear that Scarlett's inner state is obvious, that she is feeling extreme distress. However, there is no way for the viewers to know if this expression of distress is genuine. And, in fact, when the camera moves in for a close-up of Scarlett as she is weeping,[4] it reveals her peeking out from behind her hands to see how Ashley is reacting to her weeping, providing a signal that her outward appearance indeed does not reflect her inner state.

In this scene, the viewers are given a clear indication they are not to take Scarlett's apparent emotional state at face value, but in the vast majority of cases, movie viewers have no means of making such a determination

4. On disc 2 at 35:58—36:02.

Perspective Criticism

with any degree of certainty. With biblical narratives, however, certainty is possible, for a simple statement by a biblical narrator regarding the feelings of a character is a totally reliable indication of the character's emotional state.

Such a statement could indicate the content of the emotion, for example, "She feared that he was going to kill her." However, in practice, biblical narrators tend to limit themselves simply to reporting the fact that a character is experiencing a particular emotion. For example, in Esth 1:10-12, King Ahasuerus is shown commanding Queen Vashti be brought before him, but Queen Vashti refuses to come. Then, the narrator reports, "The king was very angry, and his anger burned within him" (v. 12b). With these two clauses, the narrator transports the readers into the king's inner self, thus providing for them a reliable indicator of his emotional state.

Expressions of Reasoning

Another important category of inside views involves the revealing of the reasoning behind a character's actions. Expressions of reasoning will most often be found in *purpose* clauses (". . . *in order that* he might arrive on time"), or *causal* clauses (". . . *because* she had had enough"). Inside views using expressions such as these may even make stronger contributions toward having readers merge with a character than do those already covered, for while expressions of thinking and feeling function mainly to provide the readers with a mere snapshot of what is happening in a character's head, expressions of reasoning go deeper, probing beyond merely what a character is thinking or feeling to the workings behind the thought or feeling.

An example of an expression of reasoning can be seen at the beginning of John 7. Chapter 6 ends with a mention that the Twelve remained with Jesus, despite the fact many other disciples were abandoning him. Then 7:1 reads, "And after these things, Jesus went about in Galilee, for he was not willing to go about in Judea, because the Jews were seeking to kill him." The second clause of this verse provides the readers with an inside view of Jesus—his unwillingness to go about in Judea—but this inside view does not provide a full picture of Jesus' thinking. However, the concluding causal clause functions to fill out the picture for the readers, taking them deeper into the mind of Jesus with an expression of the reasoning behind his unwillingness to go about in Judea.

Expressions of Hearing

It is readily apparent expressions of thinking, feeling, and reasoning constitute inside views, for they obviously involve forays into characters' minds. Expressions of hearing, however, are not so readily apparent as inside views, though a little reflection on these expressions makes it clear they do indeed qualify.

Again, inside views are pictures of a character's inner life, revealing dynamics not accessible to mere casual objective observers, and it would appear a statement specifying what a character is hearing relates something objective observers *would* perceive; if, when a sound occurs, a character turns to look in the direction of the sound, surely it can be concluded the character is indeed hearing the sound. However, that is not necessarily so, as demonstrated by a scene from *Mr. Holland's Opus* (1995). This is the story of Glenn Holland, a musician who leaves the hectic world of performance to take a job as a high school music teacher, hoping this will allow him to spend more time with his wife Iris, and also fulfill a dream to compose an orchestral piece that will make him famous.

The scene significant for our purposes captures Glenn as he plays his piano and sings a silly children's song to his infant son Cole whom Iris is holding on her lap as she sits on the piano bench next to Glenn. Cole looks up at Glenn as he is singing, prompting Glenn to end the song with the assertion, "The kid's a natural!"[5]

The viewers—all objective observers lacking access to the inner workings of Cole's brain—are able to do no more than assume Cole is hearing his father's singing, but they are not able to know for sure. And as it turns out, the viewers' assumption is incorrect, for unbeknownst to Glenn and Iris—and the viewers—Cole is deaf, and therefore, is not actually hearing his father's singing.

From this example, we see that what a character is hearing is something mere objective observation of the character is not able to discern. For the viewers to become privy to this information requires an inside view, no simple task in the world of film. One specialized technique designed to provide such information to the viewers is seen in a scene from *Daredevil* (2003), a superhero movie about Matt Murdoch who, as a boy, is accidentally doused in the face with a biohazardous fluid that renders him blind, but also super-enhances his other senses, including his sense of hearing.

---

5. At 40:10—40:51.

Perspective Criticism

The scene immediately following the accident begins with a black screen, and the sound of something like a bomb screeching through the air and then exploding. Then, it happens again, at which point the blackness turns into the image of young Matt in a hospital bed with eyes covered with bandages, terrified and gasping for breath. The sound happens again, prompting Matt to sit up in bed, still breathing hard. The camera cuts to a close-up of his IV drip, with a single drop of the solution just being released. As the drop hits the liquid below, the sound of an explosion is heard again, with the camera immediately cutting to a close-up of Matt's left ear.[6] It is only through this stylized juxtaposition of the drop hitting the liquid and the immediately following close-up of Matt's ear that the viewers are provided with a *certain* indication Matt is hearing the sound of that drop.

In written narrative, an inside view into what a character is hearing requires nothing more than a simple "he heard that . . ." which provides the readers with a reliable indication of the words or sounds registering in the character's brain. And a recognition of expressions of hearing as inside views opens the door to a large amount of data for the perspective critic's analysis of point of view on the psychological plane, for expressions of hearing are plentiful in both Old Testament and New Testament narratives. Any time a narrator states that a character hears something, a contribution is made toward leading the readers into having a subjective experience of, and thus a merging with, that character. Therefore, when the narrator of Kings reports, "The Queen of Sheba *heard* of the fame of Solomon concerning the name of the Lord" (1 Kgs 10:1), he is essentially positioning the readers inside the head of the queen to take note of the report of Solomon's fame that is registering in her brain, something an objective bystander could not know for sure.

Expressions of Seeing

The dynamics surrounding a narratorial notice that a character "sees" something parallel what we have just seen regarding the dynamics surrounding a narratorial notice that a character "hears" something. In the same way an expression of hearing constitutes an incursion into a character's head to take note of the *audio* data registering in his or her brain, an expression of seeing constitutes just such an incursion to note the *visual* data being registered. Therefore, isolating verbs of seeing will be important in an analysis

---

6. At 10:03—10:23.

of a passage's psychological plane of point of view. However, it is important to note that the verbs "look" and "look at" are not to be included, for as Shimon Bar-Efrat astutely notes, "An outside observer can see that a person is looking, but is unable to tell what the person is seeing; in contrast to the verb 'look,' the verb 'see' relates to internal occurrences."[7]

Bar-Efrat is surely correct in this assessment. The act of seeing is totally subjective; only the one doing the seeing is aware of what is actually being seen. Others may note the trajectory of the person's gaze, and from that, suppose whatever is in the person's line of sight represents what is being seen. However, that is only a supposition. True awareness of what is actually being seen resides only in the person doing the seeing, with objective observers limited to observing that the person is "looking at" whatever is in his or her line of sight, but unable to know definitively the person is "seeing" it.

This distinction between "looking" and "seeing" is illustrated by a scene from *Jurassic Park* (1993), the account of an island near Costa Rica that has been transformed into an amusement park populated with live dinosaurs.[8] The scene in question occurs after all the dinosaurs have managed to get free from their restraining pens—including a pack of small, but vicious, velociraptors—and focuses on Lex and Tim, grandchildren of the park's creator, who have been left alone in a dining room with an impressive spread of food. The camera begins with a shot from just off Lex's right shoulder down on her plate of food, and then pans across the table to Tim as he looks across the table—presumably at Lex—and smiles. The camera cuts to a shot of Lex as she looks back across the table—presumably at Tim—and also smiles. The camera returns to Tim as he takes a mouthful of food, but then, stops chewing and looks quizzically across the table—again, presumably at Lex. The camera cuts back to Lex who has a spoonful of Jell-O poised inches from her mouth, but both she and the Jell-O are quivering as she looks back across the table—presumably at Tim, though the look of terror spreading across her face does not support this presumption. The camera cuts back to Tim still looking quizzically across the table—presumably at Lex—but on a piece of canvas stretched out behind him, there appears the silhouette of a velociraptor.

This description of the scene involves a series of references to Lex and Tim *looking*, each followed with only a presumption of what they are

---

7. Bar-Efrat, *Narrative Art*, 21.
8. At 1:47:19—1:47:50.

actually seeing. This is necessitated by the fact that a shot of a character *looking* cannot indicate with certainty what he or she is *seeing*. In all but the second-to-last case, the presumption is confirmed with a point-of-view shot, that is, a shot through the character's eyes, revealing what the character is seeing. However, in that one case, the presumption Lex is simply looking across the table at Tim is dispelled by a point-of-view shot of Lex revealing she is actually seeing the silhouette of the velociraptor behind him.

The problem with the verb "look" is that by its very nature, it only describes what a character's exterior appearance suggests he or she is doing—the view of an objective bystander. It provides only the direction a character's eyes are pointed, but it does not provide the interior assessment of what images are actually registering in the character's brain, a subjective experience that can only be revealed by an inside view in the form of a statement by the narrator of what the character is *seeing*.

The significance of the distinction between a character "looking" and a character "seeing" is evident in an analysis of Luke's account of the encounter between Jesus and Zacchaeus (19:1–10). The Lukan narrator relates that as Jesus is passing through Jericho, a man named Zacchaeus tries to catch a glimpse of him, but because he is short in stature, he needs to climb up into a tree in order to do so (vv. 1–4). Then verse 5 reports, "And as he [Jesus] came to the place, *looking* up, Jesus said to him, 'Zacchaeus, hurry and come down; for today, it is necessary for me to stay in your house.'" It is important to note that in describing Jesus' actions, the narrator indicates only that Jesus looked up into the tree, but refrains from indicating what he saw when he looked up.

At first glance, this may appear to be an insignificant distinction, but it is not when taking into account the psychological-plane dynamics in play in this verse. By refraining from stating what Jesus sees when he looks up, the narrator is limiting the readers to a mere *external* view—the view of an objective bystander observing that Jesus has his head tilted back such that his eyes are directed up into a tree—depriving the readers of an *internal* view, for they are kept outside of Jesus' head through not being informed of what Jesus is actually seeing as he is looking up.

This read of the point-of-view dynamics of verse 5 is corroborated by the point-of-view strategy evident in the passage as a whole. It would have been simple, perhaps even natural, to have this verse read, "And as he came to the place, looking up, Jesus *saw Zacchaeus*, and said to him,

Psychological Plane of Point of View

'Zacchaeus, hurry and come down; for today, it is necessary for me to stay in your house.'" However, the point-of-view crafting through the first six verses has as its goal the establishment of Zacchaeus as the point-of-view character of this episode,[9] and an indication here that Jesus *saw* Zacchaeus would have the effect of shifting the readers to a position inside the head of Jesus, a move that would work *against* Zacchaeus being established as the point-of-view character.

To reiterate, a statement that a character "looks" does not provide the readers with an inside view, but a statement that a character "sees" does. We have already considered a film clip illustrating the act of "looking." For the purposes of comparison, we will now consider a film clip illustrating the act of "seeing."

The movie *Lady in the Lake* (1947) is noteworthy in this regard. The film itself is an unremarkable murder mystery of the 1940s. However, it gained notoriety on account of its camera work. Specifically, the whole film—except for a brief introduction—consists of nothing but point-of-view shots of the protagonist Philip Marlowe; that is, shots capturing what Marlowe is seeing, as if the camera were shooting out through his eye sockets.

So, the movie proper begins with a shot moving down an office-building corridor, at walking pace. The camera slows and pans to the left, coming to rest on the name on an office door. After only a moment, the camera pans back to the right, becoming fixed on a door at the end of the corridor as it moves at walking pace toward the door, finally zooming in on the name on the door, and then panning down to take in what else is written on the door. Then the camera pans slightly to the left, to the door's knob, just as a hand enters the lower left corner of the screen to grasp the knob, turn it, and push open the door.

As the door opens, the camera shoots into the office, capturing a woman sitting at a desk to the left of the door. The woman looks up—into the camera—and says, "Yes?" The camera remains trained on the woman as a male voice is heard, saying, "I'm Philip Marlowe. I got a letter asking me to come up here about a story." The woman, continuing to look directly into the camera, says into an intercom, "A 'Mr. Marlowe' to see you," and after a brief pause, continues, "You may go in." The camera then pans to the right, and comes to rest on a door bearing the name "A. Fromsett." The

---

9. See Yamasaki, *Watching*, 188–205, for a detailed treatment of the Lukan narrator's manipulation of point of view in this passage.

camera moves toward the door, coming to a stop about three feet away, and then pans down and to the left to the door's knob, just as a hand enters the lower left corner of the screen to grasp the knob, turn it, and push the door open . . .[10]

This camera work is designed to place the viewers inside the head of Marlowe to look out through his eyes. Therefore, the opening shot mimics Marlowe walking down the corridor, and the camera's panning to the left mimics Marlowe turning his head to check the name on the door to see if it is the office he is seeking. After entering the office at the end of the corridor, the camera becomes trained on the woman at the desk, mimicking Marlowe looking at this receptionist as he enters the office. And the woman looking directly into the camera as she speaks mimics her looking at Marlowe's face.

Every step of the way in this scene, the viewers are led to view only what Marlowe views. This, of course, means that Marlowe himself is never on screen, except when grasping door knobs with his hand, a part of Marlowe's anatomy he is actually able to see. Overall, the camera work in *Lady in the Lake* is the ultimate in placing viewers inside the head of a character.

Written narratives need only state a character "sees" or "observes" or "notices" something to create such an impression. Consider Luke's account of the transfiguration of Jesus (9:28–36). In developing this passage, the Lukan narrator has Jesus, Peter, John, and James going up a mountain, Jesus' appearance changing, and Moses and Elijah appearing and speaking with Jesus. Then the narrator mentions that Peter, John, and James are asleep, but upon waking, "they *saw* his glory, and the two men standing with him" (v. 32b).

This statement has the effect of taking the readers into the heads of the disciples at this point to look out through their eyes at Jesus and the two men. This represents a marked difference from the effect of Luke's Markan source (9:2–8). There, Jesus is transfigured "before them [the disciples]" (v. 2), and Elijah and Moses appeared "to them" (v. 4), with no explicit mention of anything they "saw"; therefore, though the disciples in Mark are made to appear aware of what is happening, no effort is made to transport the readers into their heads to look out through their eyes at what is happening.

Luke's version exhibits entirely different psychological-plane dynamics. First, it does not have Jesus being transfigured "before them," but rather,

10. At 3:56—4:56.

simply states his appearance changes (Luke 9:29). Also, it does not have Elijah and Moses appearing "to them," but rather, simply says they speak with Jesus (v. 30). The picture here gives the impression the disciples are not privy at all to these occurrences, an impression confirmed in verse 32 by the notice they have been asleep through it all. Then, the mention that "they saw his glory and the two men standing with him" marks the moment when the narrator transports the readers into the heads of the disciples to look out their eyes at Jesus, Elijah, and Moses, thus providing the readers with the subjective experience lacking in Mark's version.

Besides verbs related directly to the act of seeing, another feature of biblical narratives important to this subcategory of expressions of seeing is the deictic-exclamatory particle "*Behold!*"— a translation of the Hebrew *hinneh* and the Greek *idou / ide*, at least in the King James Version. Generally, they are left untranslated in modern English versions of the Bible, and this is lamentable, for readers of these versions are thus deprived of textual signals functioning on the psychological plane of point of view.

To grasp the function this particle can play, consider a scene from *Raiders of the Lost Ark* (1981), the account of an attempt during the 1930s by archaeologist Indiana Jones to secure the Ark of the Covenant. Early in the movie, before setting out on the quest for the Ark, Indie is shown trying to obtain a golden idol from deep within a long, narrow cave fashioned with several traps designed to kill would-be intruders. Indie manages to circumvent each of the traps he encounters, and is able to secure the idol. It is during his egress that we encounter the pertinent scene.[11]

In this scene, the camera starts with a shot of Indie's back as he proceeds through the narrow cave, and then catches him stopping and looking upward over his left shoulder. The camera then cuts to a shot from a position in front of Indie shooting back in the direction he is now looking, and captures a huge boulder rolling toward him from a higher level of the cave. The shot of Indie shifting his gaze from looking forward down the cave to looking back over his shoulder is the cinematic equivalent to a narrator's inserting "and behold!" into a narrative sequence, prompting the readers to shift their gaze to something new. Further, the camera's change in position to capture the boulder Indie sees is the cinematic equivalent to that something new supplied by the narrator immediately following the "behold!"

When watching this scene from *Raiders of the Lost Ark*, the viewers are clearly led to see what Indie is seeing—in other words, they are

11. At 9:21—9:38.

given a subjective experience of what he is facing—and this is precisely the function the particle "behold!" can have in a biblical narrative. It has the capacity of taking readers who are observing a character from an objective stance, and instantly transporting them into the head of the character to look out through his or her eyes.

This dynamic can be seen in the account of Boaz' effort to contact Ruth's next-of-kin to determine if he wishes to act as redeemer for her (Ruth 4:1–12). Verse 1 reads, "Boaz went up to the gate, and sat down there, and *behold!* the next-of-kin of whom Boaz had spoken was passing by." With regards to point of view on the psychological plane, this verse begins with the readers in a position at a distance from Boaz, viewing him as a mere object as he goes up to the gate and sits down. However, the narrator next presents the particle "behold!" which creates for the readers the image of Boaz turning his head to one side. Further, the following reference to the next-of-kin creates for the readers the image of him as captured by Boaz' eyes, the readers having been transported into a position inside Boaz' head to look out through his eyes. Therefore, the readers experience this new character as Boaz is experiencing him, and this contributes toward the readers coming to merge with Boaz.

Before concluding this discussion of this particle, it is important to note that not every instance of its usage effects the kind of shift in point of view just described. There are clear examples in biblical narratives where a "behold!" could not possibly be functioning to effect such a shift. For example, Ruth 2 begins with Ruth suggesting to Naomi that she should glean in the fields of Bethlehem, and this is followed by a report that she ends up working in fields owned by Boaz. Then verse 4 reads, "And behold! Boaz came from Bethlehem . . ." Here, it is clear the narrator is not intending for the readers to imagine a character suddenly turning his or her head to catch a view of Boaz—with the readers also catching a view of him through this character's eyes—simply because there is no character present into whose head the readers could imagine themselves being transported.

Special Considerations in Analyzing Inside Views

Once one becomes acquainted with what constitutes an inside view, it may appear the analysis of the psychological plane of point of view is a simple matter: the presence of an inside view indicates an intention the readers are to merge with the character whose inner state is being laid bare, and the

Psychological Plane of Point of View

absence of an inside view signals distance from the characters present in a scene. Unfortunately, the matter is not this simple.

First, it must be taken into consideration that biblical storytelling treats the inner lives of characters differently than does much of modern storytelling. In the literature of today, it is not uncommon to find lengthy descriptions of a character's thoughts and feelings, sometimes going on for pages at a time. This type of narration is totally foreign to the narratives of the Bible, with biblical narrators providing only occasional glimpses into the inner lives of their characters. This being the case, it would be inappropriate to equate automatically a lack of inside views in a biblical passage with a narratorial intention that the readers are to feel a sense of distance from the characters involved in the passage.

That being said, it must be added that in some situations, the absence of inside views can be taken as an indication that a sense of distance is indeed intended. Consider, for example, the account of the interaction between Moses and God recorded in Exod 4:1–9. After chapter 3 sets out Moses meeting the Lord in the burning bush and receiving instructions related to leading the Israelites out of Egypt, chapter 4 begins with Moses asking what he should do if they do not believe the Lord has actually appeared to him. Verse 3 begins with the Lord's instruction that Moses throw his staff on the ground, and then the text continues "... he threw it onto the ground, and it became a snake, and Moses drew back from it. And the Lord said to Moses, 'Stretch out your hand, and grasp its tail.' And he stretched out his hand, and grabbed it, and it became a staff in his hand" (vv. 3b–4). The passage also includes the Lord providing Moses with a second sign. Verse 6 begins with the Lord telling Moses to put his hand into his cloak, and then continues "... he put his hand into his cloak, and he took it out, and behold! his hand was leprous, white as snow. Then he said, 'Put your hand back into your cloak.' And he put his hand back into his cloak, and he took it out from his cloak, and behold! it was restored like the rest of his flesh" (vv. 6b-7).

In this passage, Moses is shown experiencing two frightening events—his staff becoming a snake and his hand becoming leprous. The magnitude of these experiences would be expected to trigger intense emotional reactions within Moses, yet the narrator does not grace the readers with even one inside view of Moses here, limiting description of his reaction to "Moses drew back" (v. 3)—a mere *external* view, that is, a depiction reflecting what any objective bystander could observe. The fact the narrator decides to present Moses' reaction by means of an external view only—thus depriving the readers of any indication of what is happening inside Moses—constitutes solid evidence the narrator intends for the readers to be distanced from Moses on the psychological plane. And such a strategy fits the context well. This passage falls in the middle of a series of indications of reluctance on Moses' part to abide by the instructions of the Lord to lead the Israelites out of Egypt, a response the narrator would not favor. This being the case, the narrator would want to keep the readers from empathizing with Moses at this point, and the distancing of the readers from Moses on the psychological plane does function to work against the readers developing a sense of empathy with Moses.

In the same way the lack of inside views cannot necessarily be taken as an indication the readers are being distanced from a character, so also, the presence of an isolated inside view cannot necessarily be taken as an indication the readers are being drawn into a position of proximity to a character. On a regular basis, biblical narrators present inside views of characters in contexts where it is clear the narrators are not intending for the characters to be considered point-of-view characters. For example, Josh 10:1 depicts Adoni-Zedek, the king of Jerusalem, as hearing of Joshua's recent exploits in relation to the city of Ai and the Gibeonites, and then, verse 2 reports that "he became greatly afraid," thus providing the readers with an inside view into the emotions of the king. However, this inside view stands alone in terms of point-of-view devices in the early verses of chapter 10 contributing toward the establishment of Adoni-Zedek as the point-of-view character of the passage. It is clearly an example of the common practice of biblical narrators to present isolated inside views that hold no significance to the workings of point of view on the psychological plane.

Inside views become significant when they appear in clusters, with multiple forays into a character's thoughts and feelings, providing the readers with a substantial experience of the character's inner life. An example of this is found in Matthew's birth narrative, specifically, in the treatment of the Magi (2:7–12). In verse 8, the narrator reports King Herod sending the Magi to search for the child reputed to be the new King of the Jews, and then continues, "When they had heard the king, they went. And *behold!* the star which they had seen in the east went before them until it came to rest over the place where the child was" (v. 9). Here, the deictic exclamatory "behold!" creates the image of the Magi suddenly turning their heads, with their eyes coming to rest on the star. This is, of course, an inside view in that the readers are transported into the heads of the Magi to look out through their eye sockets at the star. The narrator continues with the Magi's reaction to this discovery: "Seeing the star, they *rejoiced exceedingly with great joy*" (v. 10). With this report of the Magi's reaction, the narrator makes the readers privy to the emotions welling up inside these men—a compound inside view this time. Following this, the narrator reports, "And when they went into the house, they *saw* the child with Mary his mother . . ." (v. 11a). Here, the narrator again places the readers inside the heads of the Magi to look out through their eyes at the child and his mother; therefore, we have another inside view. And the cumulative effect of these incursions into the inner lives of the Magi makes a significant contribution toward having the readers merge with these characters.

Indefinite Details of Perception

From the discussion in this chapter to this point, it may appear that analysis of the psychological plane of point of view consists only of the analysis of inside views. However, a discussion of this plane would not be complete without coverage of another technique, a narrator's use of what might be called indefinite details of perception. To grasp the nature of this technique, it is necessary first to broaden our look at the concept of the *narrator* of a biblical narrative. In the years when principles developed in the study of the modern novel were first being adopted into the analysis of biblical narratives, many of the treatments of the concept of point of view focused in on the fact that biblical narrators were *omniscient*, possessing knowledge of every piece of information pertinent to the stories they presented. This observation is true, but biblical narrative critics were not overly successful in going on to explain the relevance of this insight to the interpretation of narrative passages of the Bible. However, biblical narrators' omniscience does become relevant when analyzing the manner in which they handle the *details* they present to their readers.

Because biblical narrators have complete knowledge of every detail of their respective story worlds, they are capable of supplying for the readers a precise description of each one. On the other hand, they are also capable of supplying the readers with imprecise descriptions, ones that leave the readers not quite able to make out the exact nature of what is being presented. The way this would appear in film is exhibited in a scene from *Close*

Perspective Criticism

Encounters of the Third Kind (1977), the story of human encounters with unidentified flying objects.

The main thread of the story line focuses on an Indiana electrical lineman who gets a close-up look at an alien spacecraft flying overhead one night while he is out on the job. The next night, he goes back to the area where he made the sighting, and finds it crowded with many other people also wanting to get another look at a UFO. As all these people are searching the night sky for UFOs, there appear two small dots of light in the distant sky. The camera then cuts back and forth between people taking up vantage points and the dots of light growing larger as they approach. However, even when the lights are practically upon the crowd of people, they remain simply lights in the night sky, with no discernible details of the crafts emitting the lights. It is only when the lights are right upon the crowd of people that it becomes evident they are not being emitted by alien spacecraft, but rather, by the searchlights of two military helicopters.[12]

This scene could have been produced with close-up shots of the helicopters during their approach, thus informing the viewers of the precise nature of the crafts emitting the lights in the night sky. Instead, the scene was shot leaving the details of the crafts as indefinite as possible. Therefore, the viewers are forced to experience the lights in the same way the crowd of people experiences them. In other words, the viewers' psychological point of view is aligned with that of the people, contributing toward the viewers coming to merge with the people.

This same dynamic can be found in the narratives of the Bible. Consider the report of Peter's vision in the account of the conversion of Cornelius (Acts 10:9–16). Verse 10 speaks of Peter falling into a trance, and then verse 11 describes what happens to Peter while in the trance: "He saw heaven opened, and *something like a great sheet* being lowered by its four corners to the ground." The narrator, being omniscient, knows the exact nature of the object being lowered, and yet chooses not to make the readers privy to that information. Instead, the narrator puts forth the object simply as "something like a great sheet," a description of the object from the perspective of Peter, who is not sure of the exact nature of the object. Through presenting this object to the readers in a way reflecting Peter's perception of it, the narrator contributes toward having Peter become established as the point-of-view character of this passage.

---

12. At 43:27—45:08.

Conclusion

The dynamics of point of view on the psychological plane are not as straightforward as those on the spatial plane; being informed simply that a character is seeing something is not obviously related to where the readers are being positioned in a story world. Still, a cluster of well-placed inside views can make a strong contribution toward the establishing of a given character as a point-of-view character—perhaps just as strong as any dynamics on the spatial plane. Therefore, the discerning of psychological-plane dynamics should be near the top of the list when it comes to prioritizing the steps of a perspective-critical analysis of a narrative passage of the Bible.

four

Informational Plane of Point of View

BOTH THE SPATIAL AND psychological planes of point of view covered in the preceding two chapters are derived from the five-plane typology of Uspensky. Those two planes are treated first, for they are clearly the most significant of the five in terms of analyzing the point-of-view dynamics of a biblical passage. However, before moving on to Uspensky's other three planes, it is appropriate to consider here a plane of point of view not included in Uspensky's typology, for it rivals the spatial and psychological planes in terms of importance.

CONVERGENCE VERSUS DIVERGENCE

Meir Sternberg develops the concept of what he calls the "informational axis" of point of view, an axis marking degrees of information possessed by each of the characters of a scene, with one end representing no information about a given situation, and the other end representing complete information.[1] Therefore, a character possessing all relevant information related to the situation would be right at the top end of the axis, with less-informed characters occupying spots lower down, depending on how much less informed they are. And, of course, a character can move along the axis as the situation develops, rising up the axis by becoming privy to information not previously known to him or her, or dropping down the axis with the

---

1. Sternberg, *Poetics*, 129–52; Sternberg also includes the positioning of the narrator on this axis, but the dynamics of this axis are more easily grasped without inclusion of the narrator.

Informational Plane of Point of View

presentation by the narrator of new information of which the character is not privy.

The readers of a piece of narrative will also find themselves somewhere on this axis; as with the characters, complete information puts them at the top of the axis, and limited information forces them to a lower position. Obviously, the readers' experience of the elements of the story world will be greatly affected by where on the axis they are placed. For instance, if they are made to occupy the exact same spot on the axis as that occupied by a particular character—that is, there is a *convergence* between the information database of the readers and the information database of the character—the readers are put into the position of trying to interpret what is happening in the story having access only to the information possessed by the character. In essence, the readers are forced to think along the same lines as the character—through the character's informational point of view—and this cannot help but contribute toward the readers experiencing a merging with the character.

The converse is, of course, also true. If the readers are made to occupy a spot higher or lower than that occupied by a character—that is, there is a *divergence* between the information database of the readers and that of the character—they will experience the elements of the story world from a different informational point of view than that of the character. The readers could have details in their information database not present in that of the character, and thus, be ahead of the character in interpreting the situation at hand. Alternatively, the readers' database could be missing details present in the database of the character, resulting in the readers feeling out of the loop when trying to interpret the situation. In either case, the readers will be experiencing the elements of the story world from a different point of view than that of the character, and this contributes toward the readers feeling a sense of distance from the character.

Means for Manipulating Informational Point of View

Point of view on the informational plane all boils down to this one issue: whether there exists a convergence or a divergence between the information databases of the readers and a given character. Therefore, the analysis of the informational plane is relatively straightforward, for it consists merely of proceeding through a passage and monitoring whether the readers possess

Perspective Criticism

exactly the same information possessed by the character, or the readers are aware of more or less information than the character. Following is a sampling of some of the ways in which a narrator creates a convergence or a divergence between the information databases of the readers and a character.

Narratorial Commentary

Commentary by a biblical narrator can, of course, cover any aspect of the story world being depicted, and it sometimes addresses what a character *knows* or *does not know*, statements obviously impacting the informational plane of point of view. A statement that a character does not know a piece of information automatically creates a divergence between the information databases of the readers and the character since the statement places into the readers' database information lacking in the character's database. And a statement that a character does know a piece of information means a convergence exists, since that information is in the databases of both readers and character.

A biblical passage involving narratorial statements of both ignorance and knowledge is the account of the birth of Samson (Judg 13:1–24). After establishing that the wife of a man named Manoah is barren, the narrator states, "And the angel of the Lord appeared to the woman" (v. 3), thus providing the readers' information database with the fact the visitor is an angel. The woman informs her husband of the visit of "a man of God" whose appearance is "like the appearance of the angel of God" (v. 6), and that he promised she would bear a son (v. 7), upon which Manoah prays to the Lord that he might come again (v. 8). The angel does come again, and Manoah has the opportunity to talk with him (vv. 11-16a), though the narrator inserts the comment, "Manoah *did not know* that he was the angel of the Lord" (v. 16b). Since the readers already have as part of their information database the fact this visitor is an angel, the statement by the narrator that Manoah is not aware of this serves to create in the clearest possible terms a *divergence* between the information databases of the readers and Manoah.

A little later in the passage, Manoah offers a sacrifice to the Lord (v. 19). With Manoah and his wife looking on, the angel ascends in the flame and does not reappear to them (v. 20), and at this point, the narrator inserts the comment, "Then Manoah *knew* he was the angel of the Lord" (v.

Informational Plane of Point of View

21b), thus creating a *convergence* between the information databases of the readers and Manoah for the conclusion of the passage.

Narratorial commentary pertaining to the informational plane of point of view is not usually this blatant in its contributions toward the creation of convergences and divergences between the databases of the readers and a character. And while the preponderance of commentary affecting informational point of view may not be obvious at first glance, it nevertheless functions just as effectively in controlling the readers' experience of the text.

One category of narratorial commentary that functions in a less obvious manner is the supplying of *background information* of a character. Specifically, the narrator's supplying the readers with this type of information contributes toward bringing their information level up to the information level of the character. A cinematic example of this should prove helpful in illustrating this dynamic.

Crouching Tiger Hidden Dragon (2000) is set in China of the late-eighteenth century. One of the main characters is an aristocratic teenage girl named Jen Yu who is preparing for an arranged marriage. She has been trained for the stringently regulated life of an aristocratic woman, as evidenced by her engaging in precise small-letter calligraphy,[2] one of the means by which aristocratic women in that culture were trained for such a life.[3] But bubbling just below the surface of this girl is a free spirit rebelling against the prospects of the regulated life of her upcoming marriage, exhibited in small ways—such as her abandoning her precise small-letter calligraphy in favor of flourishing large-letter calligraphy when visited by Yu Shu Lien, a female warrior whom Jen idolizes[4]—and in more dramatic ways—for example, her stealing a legendary sword and engaging in hand-to-hand combat during her egress.[5] Obviously, the viewers' database is lacking some key information on Jen's background that would explain this other side of her personality.

Later in the movie, this information is supplied to the viewers when a part of Jen's background is presented by means of a lengthy flashback.[6] The flashback begins with Jen travelling in a family caravan out in a desert area

2. At 23:51—24:32.
3. Director Ang Lee makes this point in the DVD audio commentary.
4. At 24:33—25:37.
5. At 15:35—21:09.
6. At 53:01—1:12:22.

57

of China. The caravan is raided by a group of bandits during which Lo, the leader of the bandits, snatches a comb out of Jen's hands. Jen goes after him, battling him relentlessly to retrieve the comb, though her rage against him is met first with mirth on his part, and then with kindness. And quickly, her rage against him turns to passion.

Jen stays with Lo in his desert hideaway for some time, enjoying freedom from the strictures of her former life. So, when she discovers her father is searching for her, she does not want to return. However, Lo convinces her to go, wanting time to make something of himself in order to impress her father into accepting him as a worthy husband for his daughter.

Before the flashback, all of this was part of Jen's information database, but not part of the viewers' database, and the resulting divergence had the viewers baffled by the two contrasting sides of Jen. However, with the presentation of the flashback, the viewers' database is made to converge with that of Jen. Further, this convergence of information databases contributes toward the viewers developing a sense of empathy with her.

The narratives of the Bible do not contain any attempts this extensive to fill in background material for the readers, though they do sometimes present more modest backstories of characters. Consider, for example, Mark 5:25 which introduces a new character into the storyline, a woman who has suffered with a bleeding disorder for twelve years. That much detail suffices nicely to set the stage for an account of a healing by Jesus, and the narrator could have proceeded directly to details related to the healing after giving just that much background information. If he did so, the readers would witness the healing with only the barest of information—the general nature of the ailment and its length—their information database diverging sharply from that of the woman, which would possess much more information than just that. However, the narrator does not simply proceed directly to details related to the healing. Instead, he first inserts a statement on the suffering she had endured under the treatment of many doctors, and the depleting of her resources at their hands (v. 26). With this information, the readers' information database moves from a sharp divergence from the woman's database toward more of a convergence with that of the woman, the readers now having become aware of some key information related to the woman's backstory. And this simple supplying of information on the woman's background contributes toward the readers coming to merge with her.

Informational Plane of Point of View

Fractures in Chronology

The biblical examples examined thus far involve situations where the control of the flow of information to the readers is straightforward in nature. There are, however, means of controlling the information flow that are not as straightforward. One of them is the fracturing of the chronology of a storyline, that is, the presenting of events of a storyline out of their chronological order.

Perhaps the most striking example of this in cinematic storytelling is *Memento* (2000), a film about a man named Leonard Selby who is trying to solve the murder of his wife, though he lacks the capacity to retain any new memories for more than a few minutes. What makes *Memento* so striking is the fact that the scenes are arranged in reverse chronological order, beginning with the final event of the storyline, and working toward the initial event.[7] It may seem that a movie constructed in this fashion would be impossible to follow, but that is not case. Consider the following two consecutive scenes. The first begins with a woman bringing a mug of beer to Selby as he sits in a booth at a bar. As she places it on the table, she says with a smile, "On the house." Selby thanks her, and takes a drink from the mug. An old man at the bar looks over at Selby and chuckles.

The woman, no longer smiling, says, "You really do have a problem, just like that cop said . . ." at which Selby simply looks puzzled. The woman continues, ". . . your condition . . ." Selby, trying to look like he knows what she is talking about, answers, "Well, nobody's perfect."

Pausing for a moment, the woman asks, "What's the last thing that you do remember?" Selby's gaze back at the woman is briefly interrupted by a flash of the profile of a woman's face looking through a shower curtain. He then says, "My wife . . ." upon which the woman says, "That's sweet . . ." but then Selby continues, ". . . dying." The woman looks at him in silence, and as he raises the mug to his lips, she stops him, saying, "Let me get you another one. . . . I think this one's dusty."[8]

In this short scene, both Selby and the audience are in a state of bewilderment. Why would the old man at the bar chuckle simply because Selby took a drink from his mug? And what makes this woman think Selby's beer

---

7. The crafting of the movie also involves the insertion of scenes not part of the chronological progression of the main storyline in between the scenes that are. However, it is the scenes that do make up the chronological progression that illustrate the point-of-view dynamic under examination, and so, only they will be considered here.

8. At 1:22:30—1:23:16.

is "dusty"? Both Selby and the audience have no answers to these questions because they both are not privy to what has just taken place in this bar in the preceding few minutes—Selby, because he has the short-term memory problem, and the audience, because it has not yet reached those events, the scenes being presented in reverse chronological order.

While these questions are never answered for Selby, they are for the audience in the following scene covering those preceding minutes.[9] This scene shows Selby arriving at the bar, having found a coaster from the bar in his pocket, with "Come by after. Natalie" written on the back. Most of the scene consists of a conversation between Selby and the woman from the preceding scene, who happens to be Natalie. The content of the conversation is not relevant for our purposes, but it does result in Selby revealing to Natalie his short-term memory problem, and in Natalie expressing some skepticism about it. At the end of the scene, Natalie goes to the beer tap, pours Selby a beer, and then takes the mug to the old man at the bar and motions to him to spit in it—in full view of Selby—which he does. Then Natalie brings the mug to Selby, and motions to him to do the same. After some initial reluctance, he relents, and spits into the mug. Finally, Natalie adds her own spit to the mug.

At this point, Selby moves to a booth, and starts looking through some photos he has pulled from his pocket. Then Natalie comes over and places the mug of beer on his table, saying, "On the house," and having thanked her, Selby takes a drink from the mug, thus catching up to the beginning of the preceding scene. And with the information presented in this scene, it now becomes evident why the old man at the bar chuckled when Selby took a drink from the mug, and why Natalie stopped Selby from taking a second drink from it, having to resort to the lame excuse that it was "dusty."

In essence, arranging of the scenes in reverse chronological order—resulting in the audience not being aware of what happened in the bar in the few minutes before Selby took his drink from the mug—mimics for the viewers Selby's own experience of short-term memory loss. In terms of informational point of view, Selby's information database does not contain the spitting incidences, and neither does the information database of the viewers. Therefore, a convergence has been created between the databases of the viewers and Selby, simply through a fracture in the chronology of the storyline.

---

9. At 1:23:40—1:26:32.

Informational Plane of Point of View

Of course, no piece of biblical narrative presents events in reverse chronological order in the way *Memento* does. However, there do exist passages that exhibit fractures in chronology. Consider, for example, the account of the death of John the Baptist in Matt 14:1–12. The preceding passage depicts Jesus facing opposition from his own townspeople, ending with a note that he did not perform many miracles there because of their unbelief (13:58). This is followed immediately by a report of Herod hearing at that time about Jesus and thinking he is John the Baptist raised from the dead (14:1–2). At this point, the narrator fractures the chronology of the account. Instead of continuing with what Herod does in response to what he has heard about Jesus, the narrator transports the readers back to an earlier point in time to show the readers the circumstances surrounding Herod's execution of John (vv. 3–12).

At the beginning of the account, there exists a divergence between the information database of the readers and that of Herod. As the readers are proceeding through the material presented in 14:1–2, they do so with a database lacking in information that is present in the database of Herod, namely, that John is dead at the behest of Herod. However, when the readers are taken back in time to witness the circumstances surrounding John's death, their database is gradually filled up with the previously missing information, thus moving their database toward a convergence with that of Herod.

"Experience Language"

In a 1970 article, Klaus Haacker develops the concept of what he calls "experience language," which involves the reporter of an event using language reflecting the subjective perception of a person experiencing the event, even if the subjective perception has no basis in objective reality.[10] Though Haacker does not discuss this concept in the context of literary analysis—the adoption of literary-critical theory into the analysis of biblical narratives was not to start flourishing for another half decade—this distinction between subjective perception and objective reality is actually a point-of-view dynamic, specifically, point of view on the informational plane.

An example will make this clear. In Mark's account of the women at the tomb, the readers are told that when the women entered the tomb, "they saw a young man sitting on the right wearing a white robe" (16:5).

---

10. Haacker, "erlebter Rede," 70–71.

Reference to white clothing has been made once before in Mark's gospel, in the memorable description in 9:3 of Jesus' clothes becoming dazzlingly white at his transfiguration. In fact, every reference to white clothing in the whole of the New Testament has other-worldly connotations, whether that be Jesus' transfigured state, or angels at the tomb and at the ascension, or the redeemed in the book of Revelation; clearly, this reference to a young man wearing a white robe is not intended to conjure up for the readers the image simply of a young man, but rather, of an angel. Therefore, we have a situation where the language of the text—"young man"—reflects the subjective perception of the women, when the objective reality is that there is an angel before them. This is what Haaker means by experience language.

Note the dynamics this causes on the informational plane of point of view. According to the informational point of view of the women, there is a young man before them. However, according to the informational point of view of the readers, there is an angel before them. Therefore, this use of language that reflects the women's subjective perception, creates a divergence between the information database of the readers and the information database of the women, thus leading the readers to feel a sense of distance from them.

Plot Situations Utilizing Informational Point of View

Biblical storytelling exhibits certain plot situations that routinely utilize the dynamics of the informational plane of point of view. This section will cover three of these plot situations.

The "Investigation"

Though the nature of stories involving investigations does not require that the outcome of the investigation only be revealed to the audience at the end, the vast majority of investigation stories are indeed structured in this way. Therefore, the audience is supplied with any given clue only as the investigator becomes aware of it, thus locking the audience's progress in solving the case together with the investigator's progress. And this, of course, is just another way of saying the information database of the audience is made to converge with the information database of the investigator.

Informational Plane of Point of View

In the world of film, investigation stories usually involve police investigations. However, what is perhaps the most prominent investigation story in cinematic history is not a police procedural. *All the President's Men* (1976) is the account of the investigation of the Watergate break-in by two Washington Post journalists, Bob Woodward and Carl Bernstein, and the movie utilizes the convergence-of-databases strategy outlined above. An informational-plane analysis of just a short scene from this movie will make this clear.

The scene occurs early in the movie,[11] covering Woodward's presence at the arraignment hearing of the burglars. While he is waiting for the hearing to begin, he has a number of encounters with another attendee at the hearing, trying to extract information from him. As the two men are engaged in their third encounter, the camera cuts to the front of the courtroom, where the five defendants are being ushered in. After the judge asks them each to state his name and profession, the following takes place:

First Defendant: "Bernard Barker . . . anti-communist."

Judge: "'Anti-communist'? This, sir, is not your average profession" (camera cutting to Woodward writing in his notebook, and stays on Woodward as the voice of the next defendant is heard . . .)

Second Defendant: "James McCord . . . security consultant."

Judge: "Where?"

Second Defendant: (in a low voice) "Government . . . um . . . recently . . . um . . . retired."

Judge: "Where in the government?"

Second Defendant: (in an even lower voice) "Central Intelligence Agency."

Judge: "Where?"

Second Defendant: "The CIA" (the camera remaining trained on Woodward's face, his expression suggesting he is coming to realize a whole new dimension to this case).

The crafting of the material in this clip is designed to maintain a convergence between the information database of the viewers and the information database of Woodward; the viewers only become aware of each new detail as Woodward himself becomes aware of it. And this contributes toward the viewers coming to merge with this character.

11. At 11:13—12:12.

Perspective Criticism

The narratives of the Bible also contain investigations, albeit less elaborate ones. For example, Gen 8:8–12 presents an investigation undertaken by Noah. The chapter begins with a description of how the flood waters receded and the ark came to rest on the mountains of Ararat. Once the waters had receded further, Noah launches an investigation to determine if conditions are such that they can leave the ark. He sends out a dove to see if it will find any uncovered ground, but it does not. After seven days, he sends out a dove again, and this time, it brings back an olive leaf, indicating there is at least some uncovered ground. After seven more days, he sends out a dove again, and this time, it does not return, indicating the waters have receded enough to allow for the sustaining of life.

As with the investigation by Woodward examined earlier, this three-step investigation by Noah maintains a convergence between the information database of the readers and the information database of the character—the readers become aware of the conditions outside the ark only as Noah himself becomes aware of them. This does not need to be the case. The narrator could have informed the readers before the first sending of the dove that the waters had not yet receded anywhere near enough to allow for the sustaining of life, thus creating a divergence between the information databases of the readers and Noah, with the readers possessing knowledge that Noah does not. However, the narrator opts for a convergence between the databases of the readers and Noah, forcing the readers to wait for week after week along with Noah, thus contributing to a merging of the readers with Noah.

The "Con"

The execution of a con fits nicely into this discussion of the informational plane of point of view, for a con is all about a discrepancy of information, with the perpetrator having information and the victim being deprived of it. The account of a con could be told from the point of view of either the victim or of the perpetrator, but since vast majority of biblical stories involving cons fall into the latter category, only cons of that sort will be addressed here.

With a con told from the perspective of the perpetrators, the audience is kept apprised step-by-step of each development in the preparation and execution of the con, thus maintaining a convergence between the information databases of the audience and the perpetrators. A cinematic

Informational Plane of Point of View

example of this is seen in *The Sting* (1973). In this movie, grifter Johnny Hooker wants to pull a con on crime boss Doyle Lonnegan as payback for Lonnegan's being responsible for the death of a friend of Hooker. He elicits the help of Henry Gondorff, a washed-up con artist, and Gondorff masterminds an elaborate plan to scam Lonnegan out of a huge amount of money without his ever realizing it is a scam. Well over three-quarters of the movie is taken up with the preparation and execution of the "sting," with the viewers being made privy to each step of the con as it unfolds, representing a convergence between the information database of the viewers and that of the characters involved in the scam.[12]

Cons in the biblical narratives also exhibit the same convergence between the information database of the readers and that of the perpetrators of the con. Consider the actions of the Gibeonites in Josh 9:3–13 as they anticipate having to face Joshua and the Israelite army. They send a delegation wearing old clothes and worn-out sandals and carrying old and mended wineskins and dry bread. Further, they lie to Joshua, saying they have come from a great distance, all in hopes of scamming a treaty out of him.

In this passage, the readers' information database is not being made to converge with that of Joshua and the Israelites, for the readers are given many pieces of information to which Joshua and the Israelites are not privy. Rather, the readers' information database is being made to converge with that of the Gibeonites, the perpetrators of the con. The readers are let in on the details of their scheming, resulting in the readers experiencing the events of the passage from their point of view. And the readers end up siding with the Gibeonites over against the Israelites, as the Gibeonites serve as foils for Joshua and the Israelites who demonstrate a lack of reliance on the Lord by deciding on this treaty without having inquired of the Lord about it (see vv. 14–15).

---

12. It should be noted that the convergence does break down slightly on the morning the sting is to be executed, as the viewers are deprived of two seemingly minor pieces of information—the significance of the fact that Gondorff puts a revolver in the waistband of his suit pants as he dresses (1:53:17—1:53:27), and the significance of Hooker's biting on some indeterminate object (1:55:00—1:55:20)—pieces of information that have not been revealed to the viewers as elements of the plan. Both are held back from the viewers in order to conduct a "sting" on them during the climactic scene of the movie.

Perspective Criticism

"Irony"

Irony is one literary aspect of biblical narratives that did not need to wait for the birth of the discipline of narrative criticism in the 1970s to be addressed by biblical scholars. However, neither the early treatments of irony, nor even the later narrative-critical discussions, focused on the fact that this literary dynamic is really all about point of view. Our coverage of this topic will first distinguish between verbal and dramatic irony, and then, will focus in on the latter, it being the one with relevance to point of view on the informational plane.

All irony involves words whose intended meaning is the opposite of their literal meaning. *Verbal* irony is present when this incongruity is intended by the speaker of the words. This is clear in an example of verbal irony from *The Dark Knight* (2008), the story of Batman in battle with the maniacal Joker. Bruce Wayne, Batman's real identity, gets word at his mansion that the Joker has threatened to blow up a hospital, and as he prepares to leave, his butler Alfred asks him, "Will you be taking the Batpod, sir?" to which Wayne answers, "In the middle of the day? Not too subtle, Alfred." "The Lamborghini then . . ." Alfred replies as Wayne steps into the elevator, and then adds, ". . . much more subtle." Alfred's intended meaning with these concluding words is that taking the Lamborghini would *not* be subtle at all, and because the intended meaning of these words is the opposite of their literal meaning, this is a case of verbal irony.

An example of verbal irony is seen in the passion narrative of the Gospel of John. When Pilate has Jesus crucified, he also has a sign fastened to the cross which reads, "Jesus of Nazareth, the King of the Jews" (19:19). The literal meaning of these words indicates this Jesus *is* the king of the Jews, which obviously runs counter to Pilate's intended meaning in commissioning this sign.

In contrast to verbal irony, *dramatic* irony exists when a character's words present to the audience a meaning different from the meaning understood by the character. Therefore, unlike verbal irony, where the speaker understands both levels of meaning—the literal and the intended—dramatic irony involves a speaker who understands only one level of meaning—the literal—and is shut out from understanding the second level of meaning evident to the audience.

A scene from *Shakespeare in Love* (1998) demonstrates this dynamic. The movie presents a fictitious account of William Shakespeare's writing of *Romeo and Juliet*, at a time in his life when he has been long separated

Informational Plane of Point of View

from his wife, and has become smitten with Viola de Lesseps, the daughter of a wealthy nobleman. For his play, Will casts a boy named Thomas Kent, not realizing that Thomas is actually Viola impersonating a boy in order to allow her to participate in drama, something forbidden to women in the culture of the time.

Viola discovers she has been promised in marriage to someone else. She writes a letter to Will informing him of the impending nuptials, and beseeching him to forget about her. She dresses up as Thomas to deliver the letter to him, but Will intercepts her as she is travelling by boat to make the delivery. Will immediately reads the letter, and then, the following exchange transpires between the two:[13]

> *Will*: What should I do?
>
> *Viola* (disguised as Thomas): If you love her, you must do as she asks.
>
> *Will*: And break her heart . . . and mine?
>
> *Viola*: It is only yours you can know.
>
> *Will*: She loves me, Thomas.
>
> *Viola*: Did she say so?
>
> *Will*: No. And if she does . . . well, the ink is run with tears! Was she weeping when she gave this to you?
>
> *Viola* (hesitatingly): Uh . . . the letter came to me by the nurse.
>
> *Will*: Your aunt . . .
>
> *Viola* (trying to keep her lies straight): Yes, my aunt . . . but perhaps she wept a little . . . (and then, looking longingly into his eyes) . . . tell me how you love her, Will.
>
> *Will*: Like a sickness . . . and its cure together!

And Viola continues for nearly two more minutes drawing out from Will how he feels about her, until she can contain herself no longer. She gives Will a passionate kiss before running off, leaving Will stunned, thinking he has just been kissed by a man.

The dramatic irony of the scene consists in the fact that Will's words are intended to be understood as a sharing of his feelings *about Viola* with a confidante, but they are understood by the viewers as a sharing of his feelings *to Viola*. In other words, the information database of the viewers

---

13. At 42:59—45:30.

is here made to diverge from the information database of Will, in that the viewers have as a part of their database the fact he is actually speaking to Viola, whereas Will does not have that fact as a part of his database. And the superior position possessed by the viewers as compared to Will results in them feeling a sense of distance from him.

This sense of distance arises in every case of dramatic irony, including those found in biblical narratives. Take, for example, the insults hurled at Jesus as he hangs on the cross in Matthew's passion narrative. Passers-by call out, "You who would destroy the temple and build it in three days, save yourself! If you are the son of God, come down from the cross!" (27:40). Because these passers-by are mocking Jesus, these words are clearly understood by them as expressing a disbelief that Jesus is the son of God. However, the readers have twice been exposed to statements by God—a totally reliable character—that Jesus is indeed the Son of God, once at his baptism (3:17) and again at his transfiguration (17:5). Therefore, when the readers witness the mocking words, "if you are the Son of God," they would understand them differently from how the passers-by intended them to be understood. The readers would not understand them as a mere taunt, but rather, as an *ironic* expression: words of truth coming out of the mouths of characters who do not believe them to be true.

Conclusion

This chapter is intended simply to provide a basic idea of the dynamics of the informational plane of point of view, through the offering of a sampling of ways in which informational-plane moves appear in biblical narratives. What cannot be over-emphasized is the importance of the analysis of this plane in the over-all determination of evaluative guidance encoded into the point-of-view crafting of a passage. The creation of a convergence between the information database of the readers and the information database of a character can go a long way toward establishing that character as the point-of-view character of a passage, and thus, have the readers come to approve of whatever he or she does.

five

Temporal Plane of Point of View

TEMPORAL DYNAMICS IN NOVELS have drawn considerable attention in literary-critical circles over the past century, establishing these dynamics as among the most important in literary studies. Why, then, has discussion of the temporal plane of point of view been relegated to the number four position in our treatments of the six planes of point of view? The reason is simple. The present work is focused specifically on how dynamics influencing the positioning of readers in a story world can be a means for providing evaluative guidance to them, and while spatial, psychological, and informational matters all relate to this focus directly, temporal matters do so only tangentially. Still, since temporal devices do have the capacity to have some impact in this regard, the ways in which this is accomplished need to be addressed.

POSITIONING IN RELATION TO TIMELINE

Basic to an analysis of how temporal matters influence the positioning of readers in the story worlds of biblical narratives is the observation that the narratives of the Bible are primarily retrospective in nature. In terms of point of view on the temporal plane, this means that as far as the timeline of any given narrative is concerned, the readers are positioned at a point past the end of that timeline, thus forcing the readers to view all the events of the storyline as past events. This serves to create within the readers a sense of distance from the characters engaged in the events. With this sense of distance as the default state for the readers of biblical narratives, our interest

Perspective Criticism

lies in temporal dynamics that inject into a narrative a sense of proximity for the readers—a sense that the readers are no longer in a position past the end of the story's timeline, but rather, have been transported to a position right on the timeline itself.

Significance of Verb Tenses[1]

The chief narrative feature fueling a retrospective perspective is simply the use of past-tense verbs in the narration of a story. This is a feature of biblical narratives that typical readers of the Bible would never notice since this is the style of writing to which they are accustomed, the majority of written narratives in modern society being composed in this manner. In fact, modern readers of the Bible are so accustomed to this style of writing that translators even go so far as to render instances of Greek present-tense verbs occurring in narratorial speech—what are known as "historical presents"—with the English past tense.[2]

This practice is lamentable, for it renders invisible some significant dynamics on the temporal plane of point of view. If past-tense verbs function to distance the readers by positioning them at a point past the end of the timeline of a story, present-tense verbs provide the readers with a sense of proximity. When readers encounter present-tense verbs in the narration of a story, they are essentially shifted from a position past the end of the timeline of the story to a position right on the timeline, one contemporaneous with the action described by the present-tense verbs, giving the readers the impression the action is happening right in front of them. To put it another way, they are taken from a position of distance, and moved to a position of proximity.

A comparison of two movie clips may help to illustrate this dynamic. The first is from *Witness for the Prosecution* (1957), the story of a man named Leonard Vole who is standing trial for murder. The chief witness for the prosecution is a woman named Christine, whom Vole thinks is his wife. However, Christine was already married when she went through a

---

1. Bar-Efrat, *Narrative Art*, 144, asserts that the value of Hebrew verb tenses for marking time in narrative material is very limited. For this reason, the discussion of the significance of verb tenses for the temporal plane of point of view will be limited to New Testament narratives only.

2. The *New American Standard Bible* does at least mark with an asterisk present-tense verbs that have been rendered with an English past tense.

marriage ceremony with Vole, meaning she is not actually his wife, making it legally possible for her to testify against Vole.

While she is on the stand, the prosecutor says to her, "You stated to the police that on the night that Mrs. French was murdered, Leonard Vole left the house at seven-thirty and returned at twenty-five minutes past nine. Did he in fact return at twenty-five past nine?" Christine responds, "No, he returned at ten minutes past ten." This causes a commotion in the courtroom which the judge quells. The prosecutor continues, "Leonard Vole returned, you say, at ten minutes past ten. And what happened next?" Christine says, "He was breathing hard . . . very excited. He threw off his coat and examined the sleeves. Then he told me to wash the cuffs; they had blood on them. I said, 'Leonard, what have you done?' He said, 'I've killed her' . . ."[3]

In this scene, Christine is telling of a past event from a temporal position past the end of the timeline of that event—just like a narrator narrating retrospectively—giving the details of the event using past-tense verbs throughout. By giving her account of the event in this way, she conveys to the jury in no uncertain terms it is a past event, inviting the members of the jury to look back at it *from a distance.*

Compare that with what happens in *The Usual Suspects* (1995). This is a film about an investigation of a boat fire involving twenty-seven fatalities and the disappearance of ninety-one million dollars worth of cocaine, focusing on the recollections of a character nicknamed "Verbal" on events leading up to it. In contrast to the depiction of Christine giving her retrospective account of a past event, the depiction of Verbal giving his account of a past event is filmed in such a way as to make the viewers feel as though it is not a past event, but rather, it is happening right in their presence. When he is instructed to start with a lineup six weeks earlier, the camera focuses in on his face, zooming in as he takes a sip of his coffee, and then cuts to a shot of one of the line-up participants and his attorney talking on the stairs of the police station, then cutting to Verbal walking out from behind them.[4]

Verbal is asked for an account of past events, and the viewers are not presented with Verbal simply relating details of the events using past-tense verbs. Rather, the viewers are actually taken back to witness these past events for themselves, thus transforming them into present events for the

3. At 1:13:27—1:14:24.
4. At 25:55—26:59.

viewers. This parallels what happens when present-tense verbs are used in a retrospectively narrated story; the readers are taken from a position past the end of the storyline, and are placed right into the midst of the action being narrated.

Past-tense verbs dominate the narratorial voices of all the New Testament narratives, with historical presents making appearances only occasionally. When isolating historical presents for the purposes of analysis, it is important to note that isolated occurrences of them are not significant, for the dynamic of transporting readers into a position in the midst of the action is effected only with a concentration of historical presents.

Consider the concentration of historical presents in John 21:15–17a: "When they finished breakfast, Jesus *says* to Simon Peter, 'Simon son of John, do you love me more than these?' He *says* to him, 'Yes, Lord, you know that I love you.' He *says* to him, 'Tend my lambs.' He *says* to him again, a second time, 'Simon son of John, do you love me?' He *says* to him, 'Yes, Lord; you know that I love you.' He *says* to him, 'Shepherd my sheep.' He *says* to him a third time, 'Simon son of John, do you love me?'" The narrator uses seven straight historical presents, before switching to the aorist for Peter's reaction to Jesus' third question (v. 17b). However, to that point, the readers have encountered "he *says*" over and over, present-tense verbs that draw them into the *present* of the characters.

It should be noted this move from a position of distance to a position of proximity does not contribute toward the establishing of a particular character as a point-of-view character, for the readers are drawn into proximity to two different characters at the same time. And this is the case with the majority of instances of the historical present in New Testament narratives; the readers are plunged into the midst of the action, but not in such a manner that they are led to merge with one particular character. Rather, such a move on the temporal plane performs a different function, that is, distinguishing a particular event from the surrounding events as especially noteworthy.

Having said that, the use of historical presents do, on occasion, contribute toward the establishing of a point-of-view character. This is evident in John 20:1–2: "On the first day of the week, Mary Magdalene *comes* to the tomb early, while it was still dark, and *sees* the stone has been taken away from the tomb. Then she *runs* and *goes* to Simon Peter and to the other disciple whom Jesus loved and *says* to them, 'They have taken the Lord out of the tomb, and we do not know where they have put him.'" There are five verbs in the narration of this passage pushing the action forward, and all five are historical presents. But what makes the use of the historical present noteworthy here is the fact that all five relate to the actions of a single character; so, the readers are being placed into the midst of the actions of just Mary. Therefore, we have a temporal-plane move transporting the readers to a position in Mary's present, and this contributes toward the readers' coming to merge with this character.

Significance of Extended Discourse

The sense of being moved from a position past the end of a story's timeline to a position in the middle of the action is also produced by the depiction of a character presenting a lengthy discourse. Ordinarily, direct discourse by a character will be experienced by the readers as nothing more than another action being performed by the character *back there in the past*. However, Janice Capel Anderson argues that with the five major discourses of Matthew, where Jesus is depicted as speaking uninterrupted for lengthy stretches of the text, "there is little to remind the . . . reader that Jesus speaks in the past. For the duration of the speech the . . . reader's perspective is contemporary with that of Jesus."[5] Anderson's point is compelling. As readers enter into the Sermon on the Mount (Matt 5:3—7:27), for example, they encounter in the narratorial introduction past-tense verbs such as Jesus "went up" a mountain, and his disciples "approached," and he "taught" them. But as the readers get into the discourse itself, the narrator's voice disappears, and with it, all the narratorial past-tense verbs that serve as a constant reminder to the readers they are experiencing past events. Now the readers' experience consists entirely of one character speaking, and as this experience continues on and on, the readers gradually lose sight of the fact this speech is a past event. Rather, the readers are lulled into feeling they are in the present of that character.

What we have, then, is a dynamic similar to that produced by the use of historical presents in the narration of a story. With extended discourses also, the readers are transported from a position of distance to a position of proximity, right by the side of the character delivering the discourse. And the fact the readers are held in a position of proximity to a single character for a significant stretch of the text contributes toward the readers coming to experience that character as the point-of-view character of the text.

5. Anderson, *Narrative Web*, 65.

Perspective Criticism

Ordering of Events on Timeline

The genre of story is sequential in nature. In other words, the material in a story is intended to be experienced by the audience in the order it is presented. Usually, this will mean the audience will be presented with the events of the storyline in chronological order. Sometimes, however, storylines will present events—sometimes, whole blocks of events—out of chronological order.

At first glance, none of this would appear to relate to point of view. Point of view is all about audience positioning and, as we have just seen, an audience's temporal positioning with a retrospectively narrated story is at a point past the end of the story's timeline, a positioning that is not impacted at all by the ordering of the events of the storyline. A closer look, however, reveals the ordering of events does indeed impact point of view. It is just that the impact is not felt on the temporal plane of a narrative, but rather, on the informational plane. This will be demonstrated with a look at the dynamics related to flashbacks and flash forwards, two temporal-plane devices related to the ordering of events on a story's timeline.

A *flashback* involves the insertion of an event into the storyline at a point *subsequent* to its place on the story's timeline, leading the audience to consider an event at a point when it is already a past event for the characters. A movie totally premised on flashbacks is *Slumdog Millionaire* (2008), the story of a young slum dweller named Jamal who is competing on India's equivalent of the game show *Who Wants to be a Millionaire*. Being just a "slumdog," he is not expected to succeed on this game show, and yet, he is able to answer question after question. In fact, he is so good he is suspected of cheating. Yet his ability to answer each question is simply based on a past experience of his life. And as each question is posed to him, the viewers are given a flashback to the particular experience that enables him to know the answer.

For example, he is asked, "Who invented the revolver?" From the choices—Samuel Colt, Bruce Browning, Dan Wesson, James Revolver—Jamal answers, "Samuel Colt." The viewers are then given a flashback to Jamal's adolescent years, including a shot of his older brother sticking a loaded revolver in his face, and saying, "The man with a loaded Colt 45 says, 'Shut up!'"[6]

---

6. At 1:04:14—1:04:24.

Temporal Plane of Point of View

Without the flashback, the viewers—along with Jamal's interrogator—are left to wonder how he could possibly know this. In terms of point of view on the informational plane, there would exist a divergence between the information databases of the viewers and Jamal, with Jamal's database containing this piece of information, but the viewers' database lacking it. However, with the flashback, the missing piece of information is added to the viewer's database, thus eliminating the divergence between the two databases, and also, the sense of distance from Jamal felt by the viewers resulting from the divergence. So, a flashback is a temporal-plane device that can impact point of view on the informational plane.

An example of this dynamic in a biblical narrative is seen in the account of four leprous men at the gates of the city of Samaria who are starving to death during the Arameans' siege of the city recorded in 2 Kgs 7:3–7. The first two verses set out their thinking that leads them to desert to the Aramean camp; for them, going into the city will lead to death since there is no food there, and going to the Aramean camp could also lead to death—since the Arameans could kill them—but it could possibly lead to life if the Arameans spare them. Verse 5 reports them going to the camp and finding it empty. Then the narrator presents a flashback, taking the readers back in time through the narration of how the Lord had earlier caused the Arameans to hear the sounds of military forces, leading them to think the Hittites and Egyptians were attacking, and causing them to flee (vv. 6–7).

Just as the flashback in *Slumdog Millionaire* affected point of view on the informational plane, so also does this flashback, although in a different way. The cinematic flashback had the effect of taking a divergence between the information databases of the viewers and Jamal and transforming it into a convergence. The use of the flashback in 2 Kgs 7, on the other hand, functions to maintain a convergence of the information databases of the readers and the leprous men. At the beginning of the account, there exists a convergence between the two databases, as knowledge of the Arameans' deserting their camp is not a part of the database of either the leprous men or the readers. Further, it is only at the point when this fact is added to the database of the characters that it becomes a part of the database of the readers. This results in the readers experiencing the events exactly as the characters experience them, thus contributing toward the readers coming to merge with these leprous men.

Perspective Criticism

Consider what would have happened had the narrator decided not to employ a flashback here, but rather, simply narrated the sequence of events in chronological order. The account would have started with the Lord causing the Arameans to hear the sounds of military activity, prompting them to flee, thus leaving their camp empty. Then would come the scene at the city gates with the leprous men contemplating their fate, and deciding to desert to the Arameans. Finally would come their discovery that the camp is empty. The narrator certainly could have chosen this way of reporting these events, but this version would have had a significantly different impact on the readers. With this telling, there would be from the start a divergence between the information databases of the characters and the readers, for when the report of the Arameans' deserting their camp is added to the database of the readers, it is not also added to the characters' database. As a result, while the characters are experiencing anxiety at the prospects of being killed by the Arameans, the readers are experiencing no anxiety at all, knowing the characters have nothing to fear in going to the Aramean camp. So, the judicious use of a flashback here totally changes the dynamics of the story.

A less-common strategy related to the ordering of events on a story's timeline is the *flash forward*. As its name suggests, it is the opposite of a flashback in that it involves the insertion of an event into the storyline at a point *prior* to its place on the story's timeline. This leads the audience to consider an event to which the characters of the story are not privy, since it has not yet occurred in the characters' timeline. A cinematic example of this device is seen in *Jesus Christ Superstar* (1973), a rock opera covering the last week of Jesus' life. Most of the movie simply follows chronologically the events of this week, but a significant break occurs when the events of Friday are being covered. To this point in the chronology of events, Judas has committed suicide, and Jesus has stood trial before Pilate and has been handed over to be crucified. However, before Jesus is shown on his way to Golgotha, there is a song ("Superstar") which consists of a flash forward depicting an event of the late twentieth century, that is, the spirit of the deceased Judas questioning Jesus about letting things "get so out of hand."

The fact this is a flash forward is made clear by the following lyrics: "Now why d'you choose such a backward time and such a strange land? / If you'd come today you could have reached the whole nation; / Israel in 4 B.C. had no mass communication." These lyrics reflect a time far in the future of the events depicted in the storyline to this point, a time when there is mass communication. Therefore, a storyline that appears at first glance to encompass a mere week is now shown to encompass nearly two-thousand years. Further, the events of the storyline are not presented in chronological order with the latest event—the one from the twentieth century—appearing last. Rather, this latest event is brought forward and placed between two first-century events: the trial before Pilate and the crucifixion. To put it another way, immediately following the trial scene, the viewers are transported forward for the twentieth-century scene, with the result that they experience the first-century scene of Jesus' suffering on the cross against the backdrop of a twentieth-century perspective. The end result is the viewers' database receives information not present in the databases of any of the first-century characters, and this divergence of databases leads the viewers to be distanced from those characters.

An example of a flash forward in the narratives of the Bible is found in John's account of an exchange between Jesus and some Jews in Jerusalem immediately following the report of Jesus' cleansing of the temple (2:13–22). These Jews seek a miraculous sign from him, and Jesus puzzles them with the statement, "Destroy this temple, and in three days I will raise it" (v. 19), with the narrator supplying a piece of commentary to explain he is referring to the temple of his body (v. 21). Then the narrator adds, "Therefore, when he was raised from the dead, his disciples remembered that he had said this . . ." (v. 22).

This move has the effect of distancing the readers from the disciples. The narrator here informs the readers of something the disciples will do years later—something of which the disciples themselves are not at this point aware. This creates a *divergence* between the information databases of the readers and the disciples, thus inclining the readers to feel distanced from the disciples.

Pacing of Events on Timeline

The issue of *pacing* has to do with the relationship between narrative time and story time in a narrative text, that is, between the length of time it takes to narrate an event and the time lapse of the event itself. There exists a spectrum of possible paces for presenting narrative material, and they will be covered in order of fastest to slowest.

Perspective Criticism

Summary Material

With summary material, story time exceeds narrative time—that is, the time lapse of a reported event is *longer* than the length of time it takes to report it. The main characteristic of this type of material is the sacrifice of detail, a sacrifice necessitated by the decision to limit the amount of narrative time devoted to a particular event. This willingness to sacrifice detail reflects the event has a low degree of importance in the development of the story. In other words, summary material typically functions merely to supplement more crucial material.

Obviously, there is a wide range in the amount that story time can exceed narrative time in summary material. A montage from the animated movie *Up* (2009) represents the higher end of the range. This is the account of a cantankerous, retired balloon vendor named Carl who attempts to float his house down to a place called Paradise Falls in South America by means of thousands of helium balloons, to fulfill a promise he made when just a kid to his friend Ellie.

The montage appears early in the movie,[7] following the scene in which Carl originally makes the promise to Ellie. It consists of dozens of short action shots showing the wedding of Carl and Ellie, and then their setting up a new home, then moving to their life together—covering picnics and their respective jobs and their dreaming about having a family, but discovering they will not be able to—then moving to a renewed dream to make it to Paradise Falls—with the dream repeatedly needing to be put off due to financial emergencies—then moving to their golden years with a renewed attempt to make the trip, then to Ellie experiencing failing health and passing away.

This sequence represents summary material in that story time of several decades exceeds narrative time of a little more than four minutes. It is useful to specify material with such a large differential as "*broad summary* material," and broad summary material will always function to provide mere background to the essence of the story. Indeed, this is the case here, as the relationship between Carl and Ellie constitutes mere background to the essence of the story: Carl's attempt to get to Paradise Falls after Ellie has died.

An example of broad summary material in the Bible is found in 1 Kgs 16:8–28. In these twenty-one verses, the narrator of Kings covers the

---

7. At 7:19—11:36.

reigns of three kings of Israel—Elah, Zimri, and Omni—spanning a period of twelve years. Like the montage in *Up*, the material provides only sporadic details of this twelve-year period, the mark of broad summary material.

In contrast to broad summary material, there is summary material where the difference between story time and narrative time is not so great; this could be termed "*moderate summary* material." It is not possible to specify a precise story-time-to-narrative-time ratio that marks the dividing point between broad and moderate summary material. Rather, it is more helpful to make that distinction based on the degree of comprehensiveness of the material. As we have seen, broad summary material provides coverage of only sporadic events. Moderate summary material, on the other hand, leads the audience to feel it is following a *continuous* narrative, though remaining clearly cognizant that not everything is being presented.

A helpful cinematic illustration of this is found in *Rocky* (1976), the account of a small-time fighter who is given a title shot as a publicity stunt. It is the coverage of the championship bout itself that provides a clear example of moderate summary material.[8] Our examination begins with round two. This round is given only a little more than one minute of screen time, barely one-third of the three minutes of story time of the round. The viewers are clearly being given the feeling some of the action has been left out, a feeling that is even more pronounced in what happens next. The camera captures "round" cards being paraded in the ring at two-second intervals, indicating "Round 3," "Round 5," and "Round 7." With each round being three minutes, plus a one-minute break between rounds, this means a whole sixteen minutes of story time is conveyed in a mere six seconds of narrative time. The viewers are even more cognizant here of the fact they do not see all that happens, and yet, they still have the sense they are following a continuous narrative; this is the nature of moderate summary material.

This category of summary material can be seen in Jonah 4:5–8,[9] the account of what happens following the report of Jonah's outburst at God for sparing the people of Nineveh.[10] This passage reports: Jonah's going out of

---

8. At 1:46:59—1:55:26.

9. Because the prophetic books of the Old Testament are so heavily dominated with oracular material, they are not obvious targets for narrative analysis. However, some of the prophetic books, like Jonah, do exhibit a significant amount of narrative material, and so, should not escape the notice of perspective critics.

10. There has been debate as to whether or not verses 6–11 constitute a flashback to a point in time prior to God's sparing of the city. This is not pertinent to our analysis of pacing, as so, will not be addressed.

Perspective Criticism

the city and sitting down (v. 5a); his making a booth for himself (v. 5b); his sitting down in its shade (v. 5c); God's causing a bush to grow up over Jonah (v. 6); God's causing a worm to attack the bush, resulting in its withering (v. 7); God's causing a hot wind to blow which, along with the sun beating down, results in Jonah's feeling faint (v. 8a); Jonah's asking to die (v. 8b). An examination of this passage reveals that the time lapse of each of these incidents significantly exceeds the time required to report it. At the same time, the readers are nowhere in this passage given the sense they are no longer following a continuous narrative. Therefore, all of this is moderate summary material, leading to the conclusion this segment of text functions as mere background material for another segment of text where the pace slows down to a point where story time almost equals—or actually equals—narrative time, and that is found in the following conversation between God and Jonah (vv. 9–11).

One other category of summary material needs to be addressed, and that is "*tight summary* material." This would be material where story time does exceed narrative time, but by only an inconsequential degree, such that the readers would not have the sense of *any* details of substance escaping their notice. This is technically still summary material in that story time exceeds narrative time, but it essentially has the same effect as material where story time equals narrative time, which is the next category.

In film, this tight summary material would convey to the viewers the sense they are experiencing the action in real time, though a careful examination of the editing would reveal that small portions of the action have been omitted. Consider, for example, a scene from *The Wizard of Oz* (1939), a fantasy about a girl named Dorothy trying to return home to Kansas from the strange land of Oz where she has been deposited by a tornado. The scene in question involves Dorothy, along with a scarecrow, a tin man, and a lion, proceeding down a corridor toward the chamber of the Wizard of Oz to have an audience with him.

Partway down the corridor, the camera captures the four of them with a frontal shot taking a single step forward, when an ominous voice commands, "Come forward!" at which point the camera cuts to a two-second point-of-view shot down the corridor toward doors at the end, perhaps fifteen yards away. The camera then cuts to a three-second frontal shot of the foursome continuing to take halting steps forward, and then cuts to a three-second shot from fifteen yards behind them capturing their backs as they approach the doors, now ten yards away. Finally, the camera cuts to a shot from inside the chamber, showing them coming through the doors.[11] Because this fifteen yard journey is chronicled in a mere eleven seconds of screen time—well shy of the amount of time it would actually take to cover that distance at the pace they are moving—this scene constitutes summary material. However, the viewers are not left sensing anything of substance has been left out in this walk down the corridor, and indeed, might not even notice the report of the event has been truncated. Therefore, this is an example of tight summary material.

As this clip demonstrates, tight summary material has the effect of having the viewers feel as though they are actually present with the characters, and this contributes toward the viewers coming to merge with the characters. It provides a close approximation of a real-time experience for the viewers, falling just short of the true real-time experience afforded by the story-time-*equals*-narrative-time dynamic of "scene" material, the focus of the following section.

With regards to the analysis of pacing in biblical narratives, it would seem logical that tight summary material would be less effective than scene material for leading readers to merge with a given character. However, that is not the case. True scene material is relatively rare in biblical narratives, with the task of drawing readers into events almost always falling to tight summary material, thus elevating the latter to a position of prominence in the analysis of pacing.

For an example of tight summary material in a biblical narrative, consider the account of Elijah and the widow of Zarephath in 1 Kgs 17:8–16. The account begins with Elijah receiving, and obeying, a word from the Lord to go to Zarephath (vv. 8–10a), but it is the initial stage of the report of the encounter between Elijah and the woman that exhibits tight summary material. The report of the encounter opens with a mention of Elijah coming to the city gate and seeing a woman gathering wood (v. 10b). Note that Elijah is depicted not as seeing the woman holding wood she has already collected, but rather, as seeing her actually collecting wood, indicating the passage of at least several seconds. Because this exceeds the two seconds of time it takes to report the event, this verse fragment consists of summary material. Further, the content of this verse fragment would not give the readers the sense any detail of substance is escaping their notice, meaning the material qualifies as tight summary material.

---

11. At 1:09:26—1:09:37.

Perspective Criticism

The passage continues as follows: "And he called to her and said, 'Please bring me a little water in a cup so that I may drink.' And she went to fetch it. And he called to her and said, 'Please bring me a morsel of bread in your hand'" (vv. 10c–11). This segment of the passage contains two pieces of direct discourse which, by its very nature, is text where the time lapse of the event *equals* the amount of time it takes to report the event; therefore, it would appear we have scene material here. Note, however, how the text's depiction of the woman's going for the water suggests she actually starts walking in the direction of her house before Elijah calls to make his second request. Again, these several seconds of walking exceed the mere two seconds needed to report her walking away; therefore, this piece of narration is also to be categorized as tight summary material.

It is important to consider that while tight summary material like this has the potential of contributing toward the establishment of a point-of-view character, it does not do so here. Note that the tight summary material draws the readers into proximity to both Elijah and the widow at the same time, and so, the singling out of one character needed for the establishing of a point-of-view character is not happening here. It is only when this type of material is used to draw the readers in close to an event involving only one character that it can be contributing toward accomplishing that end.

This is what is happening in the account of Elijah's experience on Mount Horeb (1 Kgs 19:11–12). These verses relate how Elijah encounters a devastatingly strong wind, and then an earthquake, and then a fire, and then the sound of a gentle whisper. The account gives the impression these four phenomena occur in reasonably quick succession, but not as quick as the twenty-five seconds it takes to report these phenomena. Therefore, we have here tight summary material, and so, the readers are being drawn into a position of proximity to what is being reported. However, unlike the case of Elijah and the widow where the readers are drawn in close on two characters, they are drawn in close here on just Elijah, and this proximity does contribute toward the establishment of Elijah as the point-of-view character of this passage.

In distinguishing between the differing effects of broad, moderate, and tight summary material, it is helpful to consider the analogy of traveling on a train through a tunnel. Broad summary material would be akin to the experience of a rider when the train is traveling at top speed, a speed at which the view out the window is basically just a blur, with only the occasional blatant detail on the wall of the tunnel—such as a large lit door—being even noticeable to the rider; experiencing the wall of the tunnel at this pace makes virtually no impact on the rider. With moderate summary material, the train is only traveling at twenty miles per hour, with the rider able to make out considerably more detail, like large-scale graffiti; the tunnel's wall is now making at least some impact on the rider. With tight summary material, the speed is down to a mere five miles per hour, with the rider now able to make out finer details still, such as a pattern of cracks in the tunnel's wall not discernible at the higher speeds, a detail with the potential of having a significant impact on the rider's anxiety level.

From this analogy, we see that the slower the pace, the more detail an observer is able to make out, and the greater the detail, the stronger the impact. In essence, this is an issue of proximity versus distance. With the great speed of broad summary material, the observer is hardly able to make out any detail, and this keeps him or her at a distance. With moderate summary material, the speed has slowed, allowing the observer to make out some detail, thus experiencing more of a sense of proximity. Tight summary material provides the observer with the ability to make out practically all the detail available, resulting in a strong sense of proximity. Therefore, the isolating of tight summary material can be important for the process of determining whether or not readers of a piece of biblical narrative are being brought to merge with a particular character.

Scene Material

When dealing with scene material, it is important to note the term "scene" is not to be understood simply as a designation for a segment of a movie, as it has been used earlier in this work. Rather, scene material is to be understood specifically as material for which story time and narrative time are the same, that is, where the time lapse of the event being reported is equal to the time it takes to report the event.

Scene material is used in the climactic sequence of the thriller *Psycho* (1960), the story of the murder of a woman in an out-of-the-way motel run by a man named Norman who lives in a big old house behind the motel. When the woman's sister Lila and her lover Sam lose contact with her, they trace her trail to this hotel. They devise a plan whereby Sam would distract Norman, allowing Lila to sneak into the house to question Norman's elderly mother. Lila searches the two upper-floor rooms for the mother, and is just coming down the stairs when she spies Norman through a window running up toward the house, giving rise to the sequence in question.[12]

Lila ducks into a stairwell going to the basement, just as Norman enters the front door. As he runs up the stairs, Lila begins to emerge from her hiding place, but notices a door at the bottom of the stairs. The camera follows her down the stairs to the door, and then cuts to a shot from the other side of the door showing Lila coming through it and proceeding across a small room to another door. The camera cuts to a shot from the other side of this second door, again showing Lila coming through it, with her eyes being drawn to something off camera. The camera cuts to a shot of the back of an elderly woman sitting in a chair, and then cuts to Lila walking over to her and touching her on the shoulder, upon which the chair swivels around to reveal not an elderly woman, but the mummified remains of an elderly woman. Lila screams, and turns to see Norman entering through the door dressed in his mother's clothes, and wielding a huge knife. But as he comes at Lila, Sam enters the door behind him, and restrains him.

This sequence is noteworthy for our purposes because the one minute and twenty-six seconds of screen time essentially equals the time lapse of the events depicted. And the fact that story time and narrative time have been made to coincide means we have here an example of scene material.

As mentioned earlier, true scene material is relatively rare in the narratives of the Bible. The only place it occurs with any degree of regularity is in *direct discourse,* for the time lapse of a report of what characters are saying will often match exactly the time lapse of the statements themselves. Take, for example, the report in Matt 19:16–21 of the exchange between Jesus and a rich young man on the topic of attaining eternal life. The exchange begins with the young man asking Jesus what good deed he must do to have eternal life (v. 16). In response, Jesus points him toward the commandments (v. 17). And when the young man asks him to specify, Jesus cites the commandments on murder, adultery, stealing, bearing false witness, honoring parents, and loving one's neighbor (vv. 18–19). Then, when the young man claims he has kept those commandments and asks what he still lacks (v. 20), Jesus directs him to sell his possessions and give to the poor, and to follow him (v. 21).

Narrative time for these verses—the length of time it takes to report these occurrences is about seventy-five seconds. Likewise, the time lapse of the exchange itself would also be right around seventy-five seconds. And

---

12. At 1:39:52—1:41:18.

because narrative time and story time are equal, this account constitutes an example of scene material.

Though this passage of direct discourse does constitute scene material, it should be noted not all passages of direct discourse do, for biblical narratives often contain truncated reports of what characters are saying, thus making narrative time shorter than story time. A particularly blatant example of this is seen in 1 Kgs 14:5, in the account of King Jeroboam sending his wife to the prophet Ahijah to find out if his sick son would recover. Verse 5 reports that while his wife is en route, "the Lord said to Ahijah, 'Behold, the wife of Jeroboam is coming to seek a word from you about her son, for he is ill. *Such and such* you shall say to her.'" The words "such and such" serve to designate the content of a lengthy speech Ahijah is to make to Jeroboam's wife, a speech so lengthy it takes the whole of 14:7–16 to report it when Ahijah actually delivers it to her. Therefore, the time it takes to report the direct discourse recorded in verse 5 is much shorter than the actual time lapse of what the Lord says here to Ahijah. And because story time exceeds narrative time, this does not qualify as scene material.

Pause[13]

Pause material occurs when story time is halted, but narrative time continues. In cinematic storytelling, this is accomplished with a "freeze-frame," where an image on the screen is frozen—as if it were a still photograph—but the soundtrack continues. An example of this is seen at the end of *Gallipoli* (1981), the story of Archy Hamilton and Frank Dunne, two Australian soldiers involved in the ill-fated Gallipoli campaign in Turkey during the First World War. In the climactic final battle scene, Archy is a member of the third wave of a unit that has been ordered to charge a Turkish position, despite the fact the first two waves had been cut down mercilessly by enemy machine-gun fire. Just as the third wave is about to begin its assault, Frank—acting as a message runner—is sprinting to the front to convey the message the assault is being reconsidered. However, just before he gets there, the commander of the unit gives the signal, and the men—including Archy—begin the charge. Most of them are cut down immediately,

---

13. Technically, there exists a pace between "scene" and "pause," that being "stretch," where narrative time is greater than story time, such that the time it takes to narrate an event actually exceeds the time lapse of the event itself. However, stretch material is not a significant component in the narratives of the Bible and so will not be covered here.

Perspective Criticism

but Archy is able to evade the initial rounds of fire. The camera focuses on him alone as he sprints, without a weapon, toward the enemy line. He is able to progress much further than any of his fellow soldiers, but is then hit in the chest by a burst of machine-gun fire, causing his head and arms to fling back, and this image freezes on the screen for a full ten seconds until there is a fade to black to end the movie.[14]

The effect of this freeze-frame is to place full focus not only on this character, but particularly on the circumstance of the character in the specific moment, in this case, his death in this ill-conceived assault. Freeze-frames in movies will often have this effect, and their equivalent in biblical narratives—situations where the action of the storyline becomes suspended, but the narrator continues to present material to the readers—can have the same kind of effect. However, such is not always the case.

Consider, first, Mark 7:1–8 which reports a controversy between Jesus and some Pharisees and scribes over the issue of eating with unwashed hands. The first two verses relate how these Jewish religious leaders have come from Jerusalem and notice some of Jesus' disciples are eating without washing their hands. Then the narrator presses "pause" on the action, and presents a rather detailed description of the provisions of the tradition of the elders on ritual washings (vv. 3–4), before picking up the action in verse 5. In this case, the narrator is using a pause simply to provide historical background material, and as such, this pause does not have the same weighty function as the freeze-frame at the end of *Gallipoli*.

Compare that to a pause in an account of Barnabas in Acts 11:22–24. In verses 22–23, the Jerusalem church sends Barnabas to Antioch in response to news that many Gentiles are coming to faith, and Barnabas ends up exhorting the Gentile converts in the faith. Then the narrator presses "pause" to comment, "he was a good man, and full of the Holy Spirit and of faith" (v. 24a). The content of this pause is not mere historical background material, but rather, evaluative material on Barnabas. In essence, the image of Barnabas participating in the actions described in verses 22–23 freezes for a few moments while the narrator provides an assessment of him for the readers. And just like the freeze-frame of Archy places full focus on him in his particular circumstance, this pause involving Barnabas puts full focus on him, with the focus especially on the positive qualities expressed in the content of the pause. Further, because Barnabas is being isolated from all

---

14. At 1:47:26—1:48:04.

else as the sole focus during this pause, the readers are led into a position of proximity to him, thus contributing toward the readers merging with him.

To conclude, the foregoing makes clear that an analysis of pacing can be significant to the issue of determining empathy dynamics in biblical narratives, but not necessarily. A pause can have the effect of bringing full focus on a particular character for the purpose of drawing the readers into proximity to him or her, but could just as well merely be providing background information to an event. Tight summary material can function to position readers in proximity to a particular character, but only if there are no other characters involved in the event being reported. Therefore, the analysis of pacing is of only limited usefulness for our purposes.

Examples of Analyzing Pacing

Any narrative passage will typically exhibit a full range of paces—the reporting of the action speeding up here and slowing down there—and it is portions of a passage exhibiting tight summary material or scene material that will be most important to isolate when determining whether a particular character is being established as a point-of-view character. What follows demonstrates an analysis of pacing in a portion of a movie, and then an analysis of pacing in a piece of biblical narrative.

The movie clip to be examined is from *Jaws* (1975), the story of a great white shark terrorizing a New England island resort. Marine biologist Matt Hooper and police chief Martin Brody join shark hunter Sam Quint on his boat to pursue the shark, but the boat becomes disabled, leaving them dead in the water. Left with no other options, Hooper decides to go down in a shark cage to try to inject the shark with a massive dose of strychnine nitrate by means of a hollow-tipped harpoon shot into its mouth.

As the men prepare this venture, they are shown assembling the shark cage, with the whole assembly covered in five very short shots depicting various stages of the process; in all, an event that would have taken about twenty minutes of story time is shown in only nine seconds of narrative time.[15] Despite the vast difference between the two, with many details having been left out, the viewers still have the sense they are following a continuous narrative; therefore, this is an example of moderate summary material.

---

15. At 1:50:53—1:51:02.

Perspective Criticism

After a few other matters of preparation are accomplished, the viewers are shown Hooper climbing into the shark cage; his engaging in some interaction with the others; his being submerged in the cage; his acclimatizing himself to the new environment; his seeing the shark approaching, watching it swim by and disappear in the murky water; his preparing the harpoon gun and standing alert in preparation for a shot; his being jolted as the shark slams into the cage from his blind side, causing him to drop the gun; his staring at the bars of the cage splayed open by the impact; his looking through the bottom of the cage after the dropped harpoon gun; his turning just in time to see the shark slam into the cage again; his trying to fend off the shark's advances with his knife; his lifting himself to the top of the cage as the shark's snout penetrates deeper and deeper into the cage with each thrust; his managing to slip out of the cage unnoticed and swim down toward the seabed.[16]

An examination of all these shots reveals that the time lapse of the events depicted—that is, the story time for this sequence—is about four minutes. This falls right in the range of the three minutes and forty-eight seconds of narrative time devoted to the sequence; therefore, this sequence constitutes scene material or, at worst, tight summary material.

To summarize, with the reporting of the construction of the shark cage, story time exceeds narrative time by a large margin, and this use of moderate summary material is appropriate here, for the assembly of the shark cage is mere background for the main event. On the other hand, with the reporting of Hooper's encounter with the shark, story time roughly equals narrative time, and this use of scene material is again appropriate, for this encounter constitutes the main event of this segment of the storyline.

For an analysis of pacing in a biblical narrative, we turn to the account of the death of King Saul as recorded in 1 Chr 10:1–6. This analysis will consist of proceeding through this passage, noting what type of material is being used at each point in the passage, and also analyzing any changes in pace during the course of the passage.

Verse 1 simply reports that the Philistines fought against Israel, forcing the Israelites to flee, and killing some of them in the process. This clearly constitutes summary material, and to be more specific, moderate summary material; enough detail is provided to give the readers the sense they are experiencing a continuous narrative as opposed to just a series of sporadic

16. At 1:51:46—1:55:34

Temporal Plane of Point of View

events, yet the degree of detail is not anywhere near enough to create for the readers the sense of a real-time experience of these events.

In verse 2—an account of the Philistines overtaking Saul and his three sons, and managing to kill the three sons—the report here again is moderate summary material, although this moderate summary material is to be distinguished from that in verse 1. Note how this verse actually designates particular characters—"Saul," "Jonathan," "Abinadab," and "Malchishua"—unlike verse 1, which speaks only in general terms of "Philistines" and "Israelites"; the greater degree of detail in verse 2 is an indication the pace is slowing.

Verse 3 relates how the battle is pressing on Saul, and how the enemy archers find him, and wound him with a shot. Here, the detail continues to get more precise. The attackers are no longer just undifferentiated "Philistines," but "archers." Also, the damage inflicted by the enemy is no longer just undifferentiated killing, but specifically, injury inflicted by an arrow. The pace continues to slow.

Verses 4–5 read, "And Saul said to his armor-bearer, 'Draw your sword and run me through with it, lest these uncircumcised come and abuse me.' But his armor-bearer was not willing, because he was greatly afraid. So Saul took the sword and fell upon it. The armor-bearer saw that Saul was dead, and he also fell upon his sword and died." Here, the pace slows even further. Still, the time lapse of all this is clearly not as short as the mere thirty seconds needed to report these events. However, it would be close enough to give the readers the sense of having a real-time experience, and so, this constitutes tight summary material.

Our examination here reveals the passage starts at a relatively fast pace, and gradually slows as the passage proceeds. Thinking back to the train analogy, this passage is like a train that is at first traveling through a tunnel at twenty miles per hour, and then slows to fifteen, and then to ten, and finally to five, progressively allowing the rider to see more and more detail of the tunnel walls. With regards to the experience of the readers of this passage, they are being taken gradually from a position of relative distance from Saul and his armor-bearer to a position in proximity to them, a clear indication that the circumstances surrounding their deaths constitutes the focus of the scene.[17]

---

17. Of course, because there is more than one character in this scene, our analysis of pacing does not contribute toward a determination of whether a point-of-view character is being established here.

Conclusion

As mentioned at the outset of this chapter, temporal matters are very important in the analysis of a narrative passage, though not that important in the analysis of point of view in the passage, and even less important in point-of-view analysis specifically focusing on empathy dynamics in the passage. Still, temporal matters do make some contributions. Flashbacks and flash forwards can be significant, but only in how they impact point of view on the informational plane. Pacing, and the use of the historical present, can be significant, but only with passages involving a single character. Despite these limitations, the analysis of matters related to the temporal plane does hold the potential of uncovering insights into how narrators intend for their readers to evaluate particular characters, and so, the temporal plane should not be overlooked.

six

Phraseological Plane of Point of View

OF USPENSKY'S FIVE PLANES of point of view, the phraseological has been the least understood by biblical scholars trying to incorporate the analysis of point of view into their study of biblical narratives. The misunderstanding has not been crucial, because the phraseological plane is clearly the least important of the five, only occasionally coming into play in biblical narrators' crafting of their narratives. Still, it is significant on enough occasions to warrant inclusion in our discussion.

At its root, point of view on the phraseological plane has to do with *speech characteristics* of characters. This chapter will first address what constitutes a speech characteristic of a character, and then will discuss how, and why, a narrator might use one of these in the crafting of point of view in a narrative passage, demonstrating this process with an examination of just such a case from the Gospel of Luke.

SPEECH CHARACTERISTICS

In the course of reporting the events of a story line, a narrator will often present direct discourse of characters, and it is this direct discourse that constitutes the focus of analyzing point of view on the phraseological plane. However, it is not so much *what* characters say that is important, but more *how* they say it. Specifically, the focus is on the manner in which a character speaks. Often, the manner of speech reflected in a character's direct discourse is not particularly distinguishable from the manner of speech reflected in the narration of the story. However, sometimes, a character's manner of speech is intentionally made to be distinctive, that is, noticeably different from that of the narrator, and from that of the other characters. To put it another way, the character is made to have distinctive speech characteristics, and point of view on the phraseological plane is all about distinctive speech characteristics of characters.

In the world of film, a classic example of this is found in *My Fair Lady* (1964), where, in fact, a particular character's distinctive speech characteristics form the whole premise for the movie. This is the story of Eliza Doolittle, a poor flower girl with a strong Cockney accent, and phoneticist Henry Higgins, who claims he could have this girl speaking like a proper lady within six months. A sampling of some of Eliza's direct discourse serves as an illustration of speech characteristics.

Near the beginning of the movie, Eliza is shown running through the rain toward an opera house in London with a basket of flowers, hoping to make some sales to the opera-goers as they are leaving. As she crosses a street, not paying attention to where she is going, she runs into a man hailing a cab, and she falls to the ground with her flowers spilling out of her basket. As she tries to gather up her flowers, she says to the man, "Look whe' ya goin', dea'. Look whe' ya goin.'" And when the man apologizes, she continues, "Two bunches o' vi'lets trod in th' mud . . . a full day's wages." Eliza then proceeds to the entry way of the opera house where a number of patrons are waiting under the cover, and she says to an older woman who had been calling to the man involved in the collision, "Ah, 'e's y' son, is 'e? Well, y'd done y' du'y as a mother shou', y' wou'nt le' 'im spoil a poor girl's flahs and then run away withou' payin.'"[1]

The *Star Wars* franchise involves a character whose speech is no less noteworthy, but in a much different way. The character is Yoda, a Jedi master, and a look at an interaction he has with fellow Jedi master Obi-Wan Kenobe in *Star Wars: Revenge of the Sith* (2005) clearly demonstrates the distinctiveness of his speech characteristics. Obi-Wan shows Yoda a holo-recording of Anakin Skywalker, Obi-Wan's Jedi apprentice, bowing before the evil emperor, after which the following transpires[2]:

> *Obi-Wan:* I can't watch anymore!
>
> *Yoda:* Destroy the Sith, we must.
>
> *Obi-Wan:* Send me to kill the emperor. I will not kill Anakin.

1. At 5:25—5:57.
2 At 1:37:45—1:38:33

Yoda: To fight this Lord Sidious, strong enough, you are not.

Obi-Wan: He is like my brother; I cannot do it.

Yoda: Twisted by the Dark Side, young Skywalker has become. The boy you trained, gone, he is, consumed by Darth Vader.

Obi-Wan: I do not know where the emperor has sent him. I don't know where to look.

Yoda: Use your feelings, Obi-Wan, and find him, you will.

While Obi-Wan's direct discourse reflects nothing out of the ordinary, Yoda's direct discourse consistently utilizes syntax in a non-standard fashion, straining the rules of syntax to such an extent that his manner of speech is noticeable as being distinctive to him alone. To put it another way, this non-standard use of syntax is a speech characteristic of this character.

Narrator's Manipulation of Speech Characteristics

The bare fact a character is recognized as having a distinctive speech characteristic is not, by itself, significant to the analysis of point of view on the phraseological plane. Rather, a distinctive speech characteristic of a character becomes significant only when a narrator takes it, and embeds it into narratorial speech, that is, mingles the character's distinctive speech characteristic into the regular language the narrator has been using in the narration of the story.

One example of this from the world of film is found in a scene of *The Gods Must Be Crazy* (1981). As outlined in chapter 1, the movie opens as if it were a documentary exploring how the Sho people of the Kalahari are different from members of modern society as typified by residents of urban South Africa, showing scenes from both cultures, along with providing a third-person narrator voice-over giving exposition. Leading into the pertinent clip, there is a series of scenes showing how the urban South African culture is totally controlled by the clock and the calendar, with certain activities needing to be done on specified days and at specified times. The camera then cuts to the Kalahari Desert to capture Xi walking alone through a grassy area with the narrator voice-over saying, "But in the Kalahari, it's always Tuesday or Thursday, if you like . . . or Sunday. No clocks or calendars telling you to do this or that."³ Note the language used by the narrator in this voice-over; he uses words such as "Tuesday," "Thursday," "Sunday," "clocks," and "calendars." This represents the narrator's own phraseology, terms he would use every day as a member of modern society.

The clip continues with the camera pointed into the sky, capturing a small airplane flying overhead. At this point, the nature of the narrator voice-over changes: "Lately, strange new things sometimes appeared in the sky . . . noisy birds which flew without flapping their wings."⁴ Note how the modern-society phraseology used in the voice-over to this point is here abandoned, as the narrator does not refer to the objects seen in the sky with the modern term "airplanes." He does not even refer to them as "objects that Xi would call 'noisy birds which flew without flapping their wings.'" Rather, the narrator himself refers to them as "noisy birds which flew without flapping their wings," thereby adopting the phraseology of Xi into narratorial speech.

This move on the phraseological plane of point of view functions to lead the viewers into experiencing the objects in the sky through Xi's understanding of them, through his point of view. And this experience contributes toward the viewers' coming to merge with Xi as the point-of-view character of the story.

In this example, the narrator's incorporation of a character's speech characteristics is rather blatant, and therefore, not hard to notice. In biblical narratives, however, the execution of such a phraseological-plane move by a narrator will not be anywhere near as blatant as this. Still, even a subtle instance of a character's speech characteristics being incorporated into narratorial speech can contribute toward the establishment of that character as a point-of-view character. Therefore, it is important for the perspective critic to watch for instances of this dynamic.

Perhaps the most extensive use of this phraseological-plane device is found in the gospel of Luke, related to the use of the term "Lord" in reference to Jesus during the ministry portion of the story. Early in the coverage of Jesus' ministry, the term "Lord" is used as a vocative in situations where characters are calling out to Jesus. So, in the context of his gathering his inner circle of disciples, when he brings about a miraculous catch of fish, Simon Peter says to him, "Go away from me because I am a sinful man, *Lord*" (Luke 5:8). Then, almost immediately afterward, there is the report

3. At 8:15—8:24.
4. At 8:25—8:32.

of a man covered with leprosy crying out to him, "*Lord*, if you wish, you are able to cleanse me" (5:12). And a little further along, in an account of a centurion sending to have Jesus come and heal his slave, the centurion relays a message to Jesus while en route, saying, "*Lord*, do not trouble yourself, for I am not worthy to have you enter under my roof" (7:6). This repeated use of the vocative "Lord" by characters exhibiting faith in Jesus establishes this term as a speech characteristic, though not a speech characteristic of a particular character, but of a character group, namely, characters who interact with Jesus from a position of faith.

The establishment of "Lord" as a speech characteristic of this character group equips the Lukan narrator with a phraseological means for manipulating point of view. The narrator himself consistently uses the label "Jesus" when referring to this character in narratorial speech during these opening chapters of the story, thus establishing it as one of his own speech characteristics; the narrator's using "Jesus" over and over when referring to this character has the effect of conditioning the readers to expect it whenever the narrator refers to Jesus. However, starting in chapter 7, the narrator begins, on occasion, to forego his usual use of "Jesus" when referring to this character in narratorial speech in favor of "the Lord." Whenever the narrator does this, he is adopting into narratorial speech a speech characteristic of a character group.[5]

Let us take a closer look at the example of this phraseological-plane phenomenon in Luke 12:41–42. Immediately following the report of Jesus' teaching on being watchful (12:35–40), the narrator continues, "Then Peter said, 'Lord, are you telling this parable to us, or to everyone?'" (v. 41). Here, the label "Lord" is used in its conventional sense, as a vocative spoken by a character interacting with Jesus from a position of faith, thus reinforcing its status as a speech characteristic of that character group. However, note how the narrator continues, "And the *Lord* said . . ." (v. 42). Instead of simply saying "And *Jesus* said . . ." as he ordinarily would, the narrator substitutes his own speech characteristic with "the Lord," the speech characteristic of a character group of the story.

In effect, what the Lukan narrator is doing here is parallel to the narrator in *The Gods Must be Crazy* incorporating "noisy birds which flew without flapping their wings"—phraseology that is foreign to his own way of speaking—into his narration. And the resulting effect is the same as well.

---

5. There are thirteen instances in Luke of this dynamic: 7:13, 19; 10:1, 39, 41; 11:39; 12:42; 13:15; 17:5, 6; 18:6; 19:8; 22:61.

Perspective Criticism

This move by the Lukan narrator functions to lead the readers to experience Jesus' response as through the point of view of the character group whose speech characteristic the narrator has adopted here, that is, characters who interact with Jesus from a position of faith—represented in this instance by Peter. In other words, the readers are here led to merge with Peter.

In working with point of view on the phraseological plane, it is important to be clear on what qualifies as a speech characteristic of a character and what does not. In this regard, consider the work of Bar-Efrat on *naming* in Old Testament narratives.[6] He considers the various labels used in a narrative passage to refer to a particular character as having the potential of reflecting differing phraseological points of view of that character. This point is well taken, for such labels can in fact constitute speech characteristics of a story's characters which a narrator may adopt into narratorial speech. However, the way in which Bar-Efrat actually discusses characters' labels in Old Testament narratives reveals he is thinking in terms foreign to point of view on the phraseological plane.

Consider Bar-Efrat's treatment of the ways in which Ishmael is designated in Gen 21:9–21: "Sarah saw *the son of Hagar the Egyptian*. . . . And the thing was very displeasing to Abraham on account of *his son*. . . . And he took bread and a skin of water, and gave it to Hagar, putting it on her shoulder, along with *the child*. . . . When the water in the skin was gone, she cast *the child* under one of the bushes. . . . And God heard the voice of *the lad*. . . . And God was with *the lad* . . ."[7] According to Bar-Efrat, "for Sarah Ishmael is merely the son of Hagar, the Egyptian woman, for Abraham he is his son, for Hagar he is the child, her child, while for God he is what he is, namely, the lad. The narrator refers to him by different terms in accordance with the various attitudes to Ishmael."[8]

At first glance, what Bar-Efrat is saying here may appear to be parallel to the above treatment of "Lord" in Luke 12:42. However, a closer look reveals a significant distinction. As we have seen, the workings of point of view on the phraseological plane have to do with a narrator incorporating speech characteristics of characters into narratorial speech, and "Lord" qualifies since it is indeed a speech characteristic of a character group in the gospel of Luke. Compare that to the designations for Ishmael cited by Bar-Efrat—"the son of Hagar the Egyptian," "his son," "the child," and "the

---

6. Bar-Efrat, *Narrative Art*, 36–37.
7. Emphasis of Bar-Efrat, quoting from the *Revised Standard Version*.
8. Bar-Efrat, *Narrative Art*, 37.

lad." None of these qualify as speech characteristics. It is only repeated use in a character's direct discourse that establishes something as a speech characteristic of that character, and the designations cited by Bar-Efrat are nowhere to be found in the direct discourse of characters in Gen 21.

Note the concluding words of the quote from Bar-Efrat, that the different designations reflect "various attitudes toward Ishmael." Here, Bar-Efrat is addressing *thoughts* about Ishmael as opposed to phraseological labels for him, and this focus on thoughts takes us away from the phraseological plane of point of view to the psychological plane; Bar-Efrat's analysis of "the son of Hagar the Egyptian," "his son," "the child," and "the lad" addresses what various characters are thinking about Ishmael, and thus, reflects psychological-plane, as opposed to phraseological-plane, dynamics.

seven

Ideological Plane of Point of View

IDEOLOGY IS OBVIOUSLY AN important topic to consider in the analysis of a narrative. All narratives will reflect ideological stances, whether expressed blatantly or divulged subtly, and these stances will often constitute the *raison d'être* of the narratives exhibiting them. However, the study of the ideological plane of point of view specifically is of only limited importance for our purposes, that is, how point-of-view dynamics can effect a merging of readers with characters in a narrative. This is the reason why the ideological plane has been left to last in our consideration of the six planes on which point of view functions. This chapter will first outline the various levels in a narrative at which ideology functions, and then will move to one specific ideological-plane dynamic a biblical narrator can use in the service of establishing a particular character as a point-of-view character.

In conceptualizing ideology in a narrative, it is helpful to distinguish between ideology functioning on a macro level versus ideology functioning on a micro level. Starting with the former, ideology can function at the level of a narrative as a whole. At this level, there could be, for example, a single ideological stance dominating the whole narrative. This is not to say this single dominant stance is the only ideological stance present in the narrative, for that will not be the case; even in a narrative exhibiting a single dominant stance, there will exist other weaker ideological stances, if for no other reason than to serve as foils for the dominant stance.

In cinematic storytelling, this dynamic is evident in a film like *The Terminator* (1984). The movie opens with a scene designated "Los Angeles 2029 A.D." depicting the devastated remains of the city with human skulls strewn about. Then military machines appear—both on the ground and in

Ideological Plane of Point of View

the air—shooting laser beams into the rubble, with the occasional figure running for cover. Over this picture of destruction appear the words, "The machines rose from the ashes of the nuclear fire. Their war to exterminate mankind had raged for decades, but the final battle would not be fought in the future. It would be fought here, in our present. Tonight . . ."[1]

This opening minute of the movie functions to set forth an ideological stance that will be important later in the storyline, the belief that it is good for the human race to be saved from extinction at the hands of the machines. This stance is established right here at the outset, and it serves to color the viewers' experience of everything they witness, resulting in their siding with all efforts to thwart the machines' attempts to obliterate the human race.

Narrative analysis of Mark has pointed out this gospel exhibits just such an overarching ideological stance, specifically, "God's terms (as the narrator understands them) are good and . . . human terms are bad, that is, 'thinking in God's terms' is the reliable view and 'thinking in human terms' is the incorrect view."[2] However, while this ideological stance is indeed to be found in Mark, it plays no significant role in the encoding of evaluative signals in the point-of-view crafting of the gospel.

Insights helpful in unearthing such evaluative signals are not to be found in macro-level analyses like this, but rather, in micro-level analyses of the various ideological stances of characters. Analysis at this level could consist, for example, of monitoring how a character stands in relation to an overarching ideological stance of the narrative. Think, for example, of the movie *Avatar* (2009), the story of human settlement on Pandora, a moon in the Alpha Centauri system, for the purposes of mining an extremely valuable mineral called "unobtanium." Central to the storyline is the fact an exceptionally rich deposit of unobtanium is situated directly beneath the Hometree of the Omaticaya clan of the indigenous Na'vi, a species of blue-skinned humanoids who grow to ten-feet tall. The RDA Corporation questing for the unobtanium have at their disposal a technology for combining Na'vi and human DNA to form avatars which have the bodies of the Na'vi but are remotely controlled by means of a mental link with a human host. Further, the corporation wants to use the avatar of Jake Sully, who has gained the trust of the Na'vi, to convince them to move away from their Hometree, thus freeing up access to the unobtanium.

1. At 0:00:43—0:01:43.
2. Rhoads et al., *Mark as Story*, 45.

Perspective Criticism

The first twenty-four minutes of the movie are centered exclusively in the RDA complex on Pandora,[3] and so, it is not surprising it is the ideological stance of RDA that permeates the opening scenes. For example, new arrivals are shown receiving warnings the Na'vi want them dead.[4] Also, the complex administrator is depicted expressing frustration that "those savages" are threatening the whole mining operation.[5] This reflects the overarching ideological stance dominating the early going of the storyline.

An assessment of Jake's take on this overarching stance makes for an interesting micro-level analysis. At the beginning of the movie, Jake's activities as an avatar are strictly for scientific research of the Na'vi, but the head of security approaches him to see if he would be willing to pass on any intelligence that might be helpful in case a forcible removal of the people becomes necessary, and Jake is happy to oblige.[6] Therefore, early in the storyline, Jake's personal ideological stance is in line with that of the corporation.

However, as his avatar spends time actually living among the Na'vi, Jake's ideological stance begins to evolve away from that of the corporation. This is vividly illustrated in his taking a stand in front of one of the corporation's gigantic bulldozers to prevent it from destroying a grove of trees sacred to the Na'vi;[7] here, he demonstrates he is no longer simply viewing the Na'vi the way the corporation does, that is, as a hindrance to progress. Still, his ideological stance at this point has not evolved completely away from that of the corporation; when faced with the prospect of the corporation launching an all-out attack to destroy Hometree, he urges the Na'vi to flee lest they be killed,[8] totally in concert with the wishes of the corporation. It is only when he witnesses the carnage brought about by the corporation in the attack that the evolution of Jake's ideological stance away from that of the corporation becomes complete, as evidenced in an impassioned speech he makes to the Na'vi: "The Sky People have sent us a message, that they can take whatever they want, and no one can stop them. We will send them

---

3. While this is true for the theatrical release version, the extended cut opens with coverage of Jake while he is still back on earth.

4. At 6:44—7:13 of the theatrical release, and 10:38—11:07 of the extended cut.

5. At 13:48—13:59 of the theatrical release, and 17:42—17:53 of the extended cut.

6. At 22:22—23:06 of the theatrical release, and 26:16—27:00 of the extended cut.

7. At 1:26:27—1:26:58 of the theatrical release, and 1:39:22—1:39:53 of the extended cut.

8. At 1:36:18—1:36:34 of the theatrical release, and 1:50:16—1:50:32 of the extended cut.

Ideological Plane of Point of View

a message . . . we will show the Sky People that they *cannot* take whatever they want . . ."[9]

This micro-level monitoring of ideology captures the relationship of a character's personal ideological stance to an overarching ideological stance of a narrative. Micro-level monitoring can also relate to what stances a character takes on particular issues arising throughout the storyline. This, of course, could involve stances on a wide variety of issues—ranging from ones that are weighty to ones that are quite mundane—all making contributions toward creating the character's ideological profile.

Consider a short scene from *Around the World in 80 Days* (1956). This is a movie set in the 1870s about a bet made by English gentleman, Phineas Fogg, that he could travel around the world in a mere eighty days, with the storyline following his exploits during this journey. The scene in question takes place during the American leg of the journey when Fogg is in San Francisco. He needs to enter a saloon to retrieve his valet who has wandered in, and upon finding him, he comments, "This is a very primate country; we are going to need some protection."[10] This off-hand comment reveals Fogg's ideological stance on Americans, but it is a stance that has practically no significance to the overall plot of the story. Still, it does serve to fill out the overall ideological profile of Fogg as a character.

The preceding two movie clips demonstrate characters' ideological stances being communicated to the viewers via direct speech. However, this is not the only way ideological stances are revealed. Another common means for doing so is simply through allowing a character's actions to speak for themselves. This is evident in a scene from the animated film *WALL-E* (2008), the account of a trash-compacting robot working to clear up garbage produced by humans, who all left planet Earth in spaceships for a five-year clean-up period. However, eight hundred years later, the humans are now still living in those spaceships, with WALL-E as the only clean-up robot still in operation.

In the execution of his job, WALL-E must decide on what should be compacted and what should be spared. At one point, he comes across a ring box, and when he flips it open, he finds a ring set with a large diamond. After examining the ring for a moment, he discards it, but being intrigued

---

9. At 2:02:30—2:03:18 of the theatrical release, and 2:16:27—2:17:15 of the extended cut.

10. On disc 2, at 11:51—11:53.

by the hinged cover of the ring box, he preserves it.[11] Through this scene, the viewers are exposed to something of what WALL-E values, and thus, something of his ideological make-up; he exhibits an ideological stance valuing a hinged box that opens and closes, and not valuing a ring that serves no apparent function.

Taking the analysis of characters' ideological stances to a more complex level, there are, of course, situations where the stances of various characters will differ from each other, thus giving rise to conflict. An interesting case of a matrix of competing ideological stances is seen in the movie *The Bridge on the River Kwai* (1957), the account of British soldiers being held in a Second World War Japanese POW camp, and being forced to build a bridge over a river in the jungles of Thailand.

It is the bridge that constitutes the object of the conflicting ideological stances. At the beginning of the movie, Colonel Saito, the commandant of the camp, is shown making it clear to the prisoners upon their arrival that all of them, including officers, will be participating in the building of the bridge.[12] However, Colonel Nicholson, the commander of the British troops, insists the provisions of the Geneva Convention be observed, thus exempting officers from manual labor.[13] And this initial conflict between competing ideological stances goes on for a significant stretch of the film, with that of Nicholson prevailing in the end.[14]

Once Nicholson begins to address his mind to the building of the bridge, another case of conflicting ideological stances arises. On the one hand, there is the ideological stance of the prisoners who had been working on the bridge, a stance that their efforts should thwart the completion of the bridge in any way possible.[15] On the other hand, there is the ideological stance of Nicholson, reflected in an address to his officers:

> I tell you, gentlemen, we have a problem on our hands. Thanks to the Japanese, we now command a rabble—no order, no discipline. Our task is to rebuild the battalion. It isn't going to be easy, but fortunately, we have the means at hand: the bridge. . . . We can teach these barbarians a lesson in Western methods and efficiency that will put them to shame. We'll show them what the British

11. At 11:00—11:08.
12. At 11:52—13:38.
13. At 14:01—14:30.
14. At 20:57—1:04:49.
15. At 1:05:33—1:06:20.

Ideological Plane of Point of View

soldier is capable of doing. . . . I realize how difficult it's going will be in this God-forsaken place where you can't find what you need. There's the challenge. . . . I know our men; you've got to keep them occupied. The fact is if there weren't any work for them to do, we'd invent some. . . . So, we're lucky. But it's going to be a proper bridge. Now, here again, I know the men. It's essential that they should take a pride in their job . . .[16]

Therefore, over against the existing stance of thwarting the building of the bridge, Nicholson introduces a competing stance of doing the best job possible, and it is Nicholson's stance that wins the day.

In both of the conflicts thus far, Nicholson has come out on top. However, unbeknownst to him, another ideological stance on the bridge is emerging, far away in Ceylon. There, Allied strategists are introduced into the storyline who possess the ideological stance that the bridge should be destroyed,[17] and emerging out of this stance, a team is dispatched into the jungles of Thailand to take out the bridge, the team including an American escapee from the camp. And the climax of the movie has Colonel Nicholson forced to make an on-the-spot decision between maintaining his ideological stance—and saving the bridge as a monument to British efficiency—or adopting the ideological stance of the demolition team—and blowing up the bridge.[18]

Determining the ideological stances of characters as we have done here is certainly important in the task of analyzing ideology in a narrative, but doing so, in itself, does not necessarily contribute toward discerning whether or not any of the characters are being established as a point-of-view character. Something more of each character's ideological stances may be uncovered through such analyses, but that does not address whether the audience is being led to merge with a particular character.

In the last chapter, we saw how a narrator's adoption of a phraseological trait of a character into narratorial speech functions to contribute toward the establishment of that character as a point-of-view character, and it is possible the logic behind that phraseological-plane dynamic could apply

---

16. At 1:08:09—1:09:17.

17. At 1:22:25—1:23:25 of the BluRay version of the movie. The earlier DVD version splits the movie in half, with each half on a separate layer on the disc. Further, the time signature restarts at 00:00:00 at the beginning of the second layer. The time signature for this clip in the DVD version is 0:00:40—0:01:44 on the second layer.

18. At 2:35:20—2:37:53 of the BluRay version, and 1:13:52—1:16:25 of the second layer of the DVD version.

to dynamics on the ideological plane as well. The insertion of a character's phraseological trait into narratorial speech constitutes an indication the narrator feels an affinity with the character and wants the readers to experience the events of the storyline through that character's point of view. This being the case, would it not also be true that the insertion of a character's *ideological stance* into narratorial speech should be understood as an indication the narrator feels an affinity with that character and wishes for the audience to adopt that character's point of view? Therefore, an ideological-plane move for which the perspective critic should be watching is a narrator's insertion of a character's ideological stance into narratorial speech.

The spotting of such a move requires considerably more care than does the discerning of instances where a character's phraseological traits are being adopted into narratorial speech. Instances of this phraseological-plane move are easy to spot, for they involve a notable change in the style in which the story is being narrated; the insertion of phraseological traits will usually be quite jarring. In contrast, the insertion of an ideological stance of a character into narratorial speech may not be jarring at all; it will simply consist of the presence of an ideological stance not seen previously in narratorial speech, but it will be presented in the phraseology of the narrator, thus making it phraseologically indistinguishable from everything else in narratorial speech.

Besides the task of noticing a new ideological stance in narratorial speech, there is the additional task of recognizing it as an ideological stance *of a particular character*. For this to be possible, the expression of the character's ideological stance must be prominent enough to have made an impression on the readers capable of surviving what might be numerous chapters of material before that stance makes an appearance in narratorial speech.[19]

A clear example of this ideological-plane dynamic is found in John's gospel. In 3:14–15, Jesus is depicted as saying, "And just as Moses lifted up the serpent in the wilderness, thus it is necessary for the Son of Man to be lifted up, so that all who *believe* in him might have eternal *life*." Here,

---

19. With the proliferation of aids such as cross-references and concordances for making these types of connections, it is easy to lose sight of the fact that stories by their very nature are intended to be sequential and uni-directional experiences. This being the case, readers should be conceived of being limited to a single pass over the material making up a story—carrying forward only what has made a strong enough impression to stick in their minds—and not being able to refer back to earlier material beyond what their recollection is able to hold.

we have an expression of an ideological stance of Jesus, that belief results in life. Two chapters later, in the context of responding to some Jews who want to kill him because they understand him as claiming equality with God, Jesus again expresses the connection between belief and life: "Truly, truly, I say to you that the one who hears my word and *believes* the one who sent me has eternal *life* . . ." (5:24). One chapter later, in his discourse on being the bread of life, he says, "For this is the will of my father, that all who see the son and *believe* in him might have eternal *life* . . ." (6:40). And in the same context, he again asserts, "Truly, truly, I say to you, the one who *believes* has eternal *life*" (6:47). These four statements by Jesus clearly establish in the readers' minds the idea of believing leading to life as one of his ideological stances.[20]

Fast-forwarding to near the end of the narrative, the readers there encounter the following statement by the narrator: "These things have been written in order that you might *believe* that Jesus is the Christ, the Son of God, and that through *believing*, you might have *life*" (20:31). Here, the narrator expresses in narratorial speech the same idea established as one of Jesus' ideological stances earlier in the narrative, and by doing so, adopts this ideological stance of Jesus as his own, thus contributing toward the readers' merging with Jesus.

---

20. It is possible 3:16 constitutes a fifth expression of this ideological stance—"For God so loved the world that he gave his only begotten son in order that all who *believe* in him might not perish, but might have eternal *life*"—but it is not clear whether this is intended as a statement by Jesus or a statement by the narrator.

eight

When the Planes Concur . . . and When They Do Not

The preceding chapters set out the various factors relevant to the functioning of point of view on each of six distinct planes, but the discussions of these factors have only incidentally addressed their significance to the interpretation of the narrative passages in which they appear. This chapter is devoted to this very issue, focusing especially on the effect of having the point-of-view strategies on all the planes concur with each other, but also addressing the effect of nonconcurrence between the strategies on one plane and the strategies on another.

Concurrence of Planes

We have just covered the point-of-view dynamics that can contribute toward readers merging with a particular character, or can contribute toward readers becoming distanced from him or her. Obviously, the achieving of either of these ends is most effectively accomplished by having the point-of-view dynamics on every plane in play all working in the same direction. However, it is not necessary to have point-of-view devices on all six planes working together in a given text to effect definitively a merging or a distancing; devices on a mere two or three planes will usually be sufficient. The crucial point is there must not be anything on even one plane working at cross-purposes.

Concurrence Effecting a Merging

A cinematic example of a concurrence of point-of-view dynamics on multiple planes working toward a merging of viewer and character has already been demonstrated with the clip from *Butch Cassidy and the Sundance Kid* set out in the first chapter. A detailed analysis of the point-of-view moves on the various planes in play in the clip will be the focus of the next chapter.

A biblical example of point-of-view dynamics on multiple planes working together to bring the readers to merge with a particular character can be seen in the account in Gen 32:3–30 of the meeting between Jacob and Esau. This passage chronicles events leading up to the meeting of these two characters, and the point-of-view dynamics on a number of the planes all function to lead the readers to experience these events through Jacob's point of view.

With regards to the material covering the two characters' travels toward the site of the meeting, the narrator's spatial-plane options include: 1) shifting the readers back and forth between positions at the sides of Jacob and of Esau; 2) maintaining a position consistently at the side of Jacob; or 3) maintaining a position at the side of Esau. A look through 32:3–30 (32:4–31 in the Hebrew text) reveals the narrator chooses to keep the readers constantly at the side of Jacob. The reports of this passage—of Jacob sending messengers to seek favor with Esau (vv. 3–5); of the messengers returning with the news Esau is coming with four hundred men (v. 6); of Jacob dividing his people into two companies (vv. 7–8); of him praying to God for delivery from Esau's hand (vv. 9–12); of him arranging and sending a gift to Esau (vv. 13–21); of him sending his family to a new location (vv. 22–23); and of him encountering a heavenly being (vv. 24–30)—all maintain the readers in a proximal position to Jacob, never once transporting them over to Esau's camp for even a glimpse of him as he approaches the meeting place. This spatial-plane move contributes strongly toward having the readers come to merge with Jacob.

In addition, dynamics on the informational plane lead the readers toward the same end. When verses 3–6 speak of Jacob sending messengers ahead to seek favor for himself from Esau, and of the messengers returning and reporting only that Esau is coming to meet him with four hundred men, the information databases of the readers and Jacob converge; with the limited scope of the messengers' report, Jacob is not privy to Esau's intentions, and neither are the readers. Further, this convergence of databases is maintained throughout the whole rest of the passage as Jacob, and the readers, remain in the dark regarding Esau's attitude toward Jacob. This also contributes toward the readers coming to merge with Jacob.

Psychological-plane dynamics also make a contribution toward this end. Verse 7a indicates that when the messengers give the report of Esau coming with four hundred men, Jacob is *very afraid* and *distressed*—a compound inside view. And later, when Jacob is shown giving instructions to the servants he is sending ahead with gifts for Esau, the narrator interjects Jacob is thinking the gifts might appease Esau so that he might find favor in Esau's eyes (v. 20a)—another inside view. Clearly, these psychological-plane dynamics are not as prominent as the point-of-view dynamics on the spatial and informational planes, but they still constitute more contributing factors working in the same direction as those on the other planes, resulting in a coordinated front designed to have the readers come to consider Jacob as the point-of-view character of this passage.

The foregoing is intended to demonstrate a thoroughgoing effort by a narrator to have readers merge with a particular character. Sometimes, however, the point-of-view dynamics on different planes are made to concur in a less thoroughgoing manner, involving the concurrence of dynamics on just two planes. Consider, for example, the account in Mark 3:1–5 of Jesus healing a man with a withered hand. With regards to point of view on the temporal plane, it is important to note the narrator uses the historical present three times in this passage. After establishing that Pharisees are watching Jesus to see if he will heal the man on the Sabbath, the narrator reports, "And he *says* to the man who had the withered hand, 'Come into our midst.' And he *says* to them, 'Is it lawful to do good or to do bad on the Sabbath, to save life or to kill?' And they were silent. And looking around at them with anger, being grieved at their hardness of heart, he *says* to the man, 'Stretch out your hand' . . ." (vv. 3–5). As we saw back in chapter 5, the repeated use of the historical present has the effect of transporting the readers from a vantage point past the end of the time line of a story to a point right on the time line to experience what is being reported not as past events, but as contemporaneous ones. Therefore, the readers are here being plunged into the middle of this healing story. However, this move does not by itself contribute toward the readers coming to merge with a particular character, for the readers have been brought into proximity to multiple characters: Jesus, the man with the withered hand, and the Pharisees.

In a situation such as this, point-of-view dynamics on another plane can work together with these dynamics on the temporal plane to draw the

When the Planes Concur . . . and When They Do Not

readers into proximity to a particular character, thus contributing toward a merging of the readers with that character. Note that when the narrator speaks of Jesus looking around at the Pharisees, he mentions Jesus does so *with anger*, and adds that he is *grieved* at their hardness of heart. We have here a compound inside view into the emotions of Jesus, and as we saw back in chapter 3, inside views contribute toward readers coming to merge with the character whose inner life is being laid bare. Therefore, while the dynamics on the temporal plane of point of view draw the readers into proximity with all the characters in this scene, dynamics on the psychological plane draw the readers into proximity with Jesus only, thus isolating him as the point-of-view character of this passage.

Concurrence Effecting a Distancing

A concurrence of point-of-view dynamics on multiple planes working toward having the readers feel a sense of distance from a particular character is evident in the animated classic *Shrek* (2001). The storyline revolves around three main characters—Shrek, Donkey, and Princess Fiona—though Fiona only becomes active in the storyline thirty-five minutes into the movie. Up to that point, the story follows the ogre Shrek as he deals with: the incursion into his swamp of scores of fairy-tale characters and a talking donkey; a local lord who promises to get rid of the intruders if Shrek rescues Princess Fiona from captivity in a far-away castle; the nonstop nattering of Donkey as they journey to the castle; and a fire-breathing dragon in the castle guarding the princess.

During this opening portion of the movie, the viewers could have been shifted back and forth between watching what Shrek and Donkey are up to and what is happening with Fiona, but the storyline does not develop in this fashion. Rather, the viewers' exposure to Fiona is limited to a couple of mere references to her. In terms of point of view on the spatial plane, the viewers are never placed in proximity to her. In fact, it would appear efforts are made to keep the viewers away from her. First, despite the fact Fiona becomes the focus of the storyline from the nineteenth minute forward—through her being chosen in a *Dating Game*-style selection process by the lord seeking a princess to marry; then through a tournament conducted to determine who will go to rescue her and bring her back for the wedding; then through the journey by Shrek and Donkey to win her freedom—the viewers are never once transported into her presence to see her firsthand.

Perspective Criticism

Even after Shrek has reached the castle and has spotted in the distance the window of the room in which Fiona is being held,[1] the viewers are not taken into that room into the presence of Fiona. And even when Shrek is flung by the dragon through the air and crashes through the roof of the room into the presence of Fiona—providing the opportunity to see the princess in action—the camera is in the room for only one second before returning to the dragon.[2] All these moves on the spatial plane function to keep the viewers distanced from Princess Fiona during this opening thirty-five minute segment of the movie.

This insulation from Fiona also affects dynamics on other planes of point of view as well. The fact Fiona is kept from the viewers means they have no opportunity to receive indications of her inner state, thus distancing the viewers from her on the psychological plane.

As far as the informational plane is concerned, there exists an almost complete divergence between the information databases of the viewers and Fiona. That Fiona is being held captive in a castle guarded by a fire-breathing dragon is information common to the databases of the viewers and Fiona. However, beyond that, there is no other information common to both databases, as Fiona's database contains none of the information the viewers have been accumulating, and the viewer's database has been deprived of the information that would be part of Fiona's database. On the informational plane also, the viewers are distanced from this character.

The biblical passage of Jesus and Zacchaeus in Luke 19:1–10 exhibits a concurrence of point-of-view dynamics on multiple planes working to distance the readers from a particular character. By this time in the storyline, Jesus has acted as the point-of-view character so often the readers would expect him to play that role in any passage in which he appears. Therefore, the establishment of any other character as a point-of-view character would not only take point-of-view moves leading the readers to merge with that character, but also, moves working to distance the readers from Jesus. In Luke 19:1–10, such distancing efforts are evident in the point-of-view moves on various planes drawing the readers away from Jesus.

The passage begins with a mention of Jesus entering and passing through Jericho. It should be noted, however, that only this bare mention is given, with no details provided, thus yielding nothing more than a picture

---

1. At 33:10.
2. At 33:59.

of a nondescript figure moving in the distance; therefore, on the spatial plane, the readers are being distanced from Jesus. Also on the spatial plane, verse 2 sees the camera completely leave Jesus to take up a position in proximity to Zacchaeus, staying in proximity to him through verse 4 while Jesus remains absent from the scene. This removal of Jesus from the scene contributes further to the readers coming to sense a distance from him.

This three-verse absence also has implications for point of view on the informational plane, for the readers' information database diverges further and further from that of Jesus, as more and more detail on Zacchaeus is added to their database, but not to Jesus' database. As a result, the readers are distanced from Jesus on this plane as well.

With regards to the psychological plane, a point-of-view move is executed in verse 5 that functions to keep the readers outside the head of Jesus. It occurs at a point in the storyline when Jesus reaches the tree in which Zacchaeus is perched. Here, the narrator reports that Jesus "looked up," but does not report what Jesus saw when he looked up. This is significant because a report of what Jesus saw would have taken the readers inside Jesus' head to look out through his eyes, and this inside view would have contributed toward bringing the readers into proximity to Jesus. However, the narrator does not report this, but rather, simply states Jesus looked up, thus keeping the readers on the outside of Jesus, a further contribution toward distancing the readers from him.[3]

To summarize, point-of-view moves are made on the spatial, informational, and psychological planes contributing toward the readers coming to feel distanced from Jesus in this passage. A comprehensive perspective-critical analysis of this episode indicates the narrator wants to establish Zacchaeus as the point-of-view character of the passage,[4] and this being the case, it is prudent on the narrator's part to work toward distancing the readers from Jesus, since their inclination to consider him the point-of-view character of the passage would be strong.

---

3. For further discussion on this point, see the section entitled "Expressions of Seeing" in chapter 3 of the present work.

4. For a comprehensive analysis of all the point-of-view moves contributing toward this end, see Yamasaki, *Watching*, 188–205.

Perspective Criticism

Nonconcurrence between Planes

The discussion thus far in this chapter has focused on the two extremes of point-of-view crafting: concurrence of planes working toward merging the readers with a character, and concurrence of planes working toward distancing. It is important to consider the possibility of nonconcurrence of planes as well, that is, point-of-view dynamics on one plane working toward merging, but dynamics on another working toward distancing.

A nonconcurrence of planes has the effect of giving the readers a sense of distance from the characters involved in the action, though not to the "pulling the readers away" extent a concurrence of distancing dynamics on various planes would produce. Rather, it is more a "not allowing the readers to draw near" type of distancing. Therefore, the readers do not end up negatively inclined toward a character; instead, they are merely kept from becoming positively inclined toward him or her.

At first glance, it may appear that dynamics with such minor implications are not worth considering. A closer look, however, reveals that noteworthy effects emerge when point-of-view dynamics on certain planes clash with each other. We will consider the details of two such clashes.

Proximity on Spatial Plane / Distance on Psychological Plane

Proximity on the spatial plane would, of course, occur when an audience is led to follow a particular character for a significant stretch of a narrative. However, an interesting dynamic arises when this is coupled with distance on the psychological plane. Such distance results from the audience being denied any access to the character's inner life. Therefore, while the members of the audience are led to watch the character's every action, they are given no indication of what fuels those actions. To them, the character is an *enigma*.

Consider, for example, the movie *Casablanca* (1942), the account of refugees from German-occupied nations during the Second World War congregating in Casablanca, Morocco, seeking exit visas to facilitate their flight to safety. Most of the movie takes place in Rick's Café Americain, a nightclub in Casablanca run by American ex-patriot Rick Blaine. Rick is the protagonist of the story, though he does not actually make his first appearance until nearly the nine-minute mark of the film, the initial segment of the movie occupied with acquainting the audience with the geo-political background to the storyline. However, once Rick does appear, the camera follows him almost continuously for the whole rest of the movie, leaving his presence for only brief stretches here and there. It is a segment early in the movie that is relevant for our present purposes.[5]

This segment serves to introduce the audience to Rick through displaying the ways in which he interacts with various visitors to his establishment. One striking feature of Rick is his demeanor. Despite the fact he operates a thriving business and many of his customers want the opportunity to meet him, he comes across as sullen for almost the whole of this segment of the movie, able to do nothing more than crack a half-smile or a bit of a chuckle on just a couple of occasions.

Further, he comes across as unfeeling to the point of rudeness to those who approach him. For example, when at the bar, a woman—with whom he has obviously had a relationship—tries to talk to him, but he only answers her curtly, without even the courtesy of turning to face her as he does so. Later, when informed by the police captain there would be an arrest later that evening, he merely answers, "I stick my neck out for no one." And when the man being arrested—someone Rick obviously knows well—tries to escape, he runs into Rick and begs for him to hide him, but Rick just responds, "You can't get away," and steps back to allow the police to seize him. Another of the patrons, having witnessed this, says to Rick, "When they come to get me, Rick, I hope you will be more of a help," to which Rick reiterates, "I stick out my neck for nobody."

He is equally aloof when it comes to the politically charged dynamics flowing through his establishment. His place is known as a hot-bed for black-market dealing in exit visas, yet Rick shows no empathy for any of his patrons desperate to obtain one. When he is visited by some German officials, and has to face a barrage of questions designed to reveal where his sentiments lie, he finally gets up from the table, and says, "Excuse me, gentlemen, your business is politics; mine is running a saloon," and walks away.

The police captain puts it well when he observes Rick has a "cynical shell." However, the captain continues by suggesting he is, at heart, a sentimentalist, noting he had in the past run guns to Ethiopia and had fought in Spain on the Loyalists' side. What has turned a fervent freedom-fighter into such a cynic, not caring for anyone but himself? This will be revealed later in the movie, but for now, the viewers are left totally in the dark. They have

---

5. The relevant segment is found at 8:51—25:14.

been led to follow this character around, but have been deprived of any glimpses into the workings of his mind that would provide clues as to what has given rise to his cynicism. This distance from Rick on the psychological plane has led the viewers to see him as an enigma.

A biblical example of this enigma dynamic is found in the person of the Levite covered in Judg 19:1–21. Verse 1 of this passage places the readers in proximity to a certain Levite residing in the hill country of Ephraim who takes for himself a concubine. In verse 2, the readers are removed from the presence of this Levite as they are led to follow his concubine as she leaves him, returns to her father's house in Bethlehem, and stays there for four months. But after this, the readers are positioned back at the Levite's side, and are maintained in that position of proximity for the next twenty verses as the Levite comes with a servant for his concubine, faces persuasion by her father day after day not to leave (vv. 3–9), finally succeeds in leaving and journeying to Gibeah to spend the night there (vv. 10–15), and finds lodging for the night with an old man of Gibeah (vv. 16–21).

Ordinarily, following a particular character for twenty verses like this would result in the readers coming to merge with him. However, that does not happen here, but rather, the readers remain distanced from him. Why? Despite the fact the readers are constantly at his side, he remains an enigma to them due to the fact they are forced to follow this character with next to no information on what is going on inside of him. In verse 3, the readers are informed of his motive for setting out after his concubine who has left him: to speak tenderly to her in order to bring her back. But the next nineteen verses are totally bereft of any glimpses into his inner life.

This is most evident in the interaction between the Levite and the concubine's father. Verses 5–8 set out a series of attempts by the Levite to leave his father-in-law's house, each met with exhortations by his father-in-law to stay. With each of these attempts, the readers are shown that the Levite stays, but they are not actually told he *decided* to stay—a look into his thinking processes—nor are they told how the Levite *felt* about the invitations to stay—a look into his emotions. The readers are kept by the side of the Levite, but totally on the outside of him, relegated to the position of mere objective observers, a position from which they can see what the Levite is doing, but from which they are left without any idea of why he is acting in the way he is. To the readers, the Levite is an enigma.

When the Planes Concur... and When They Do Not

Proximity on Psychological Plane / Distance on Informational Plane

Proximity on the psychological plane generally involves the provision of multiple inside views of a character, making an audience privy to the inner workings of him or her. And as we saw in chapter 3 of the present work, this makes a strong contribution toward the audience coming to merge with the character. However, if this provision of multiple inside views is coupled with the audience being given pieces of information the character does not possess, the resulting divergence of the information database of the readers from the information database of the character is fatal to any chance of the audience coming to merge with the character.

If such a divergence on the informational plane has such a distancing effect on the audience, why would a narrator ever consider matching it with the proximity-building contribution of multiple inside views on the psychological plane? A narrator may wish to present this combination to an audience in order to produce *dramatic irony*.

This topic was covered at the end of chapter 4 where it was explained that dramatic irony occurs when a character's words are understood by the audience to have meaning opposite from the meaning understood by the character. By way of contrast, the present discussion addresses how dramatic irony relates to the psychological plane of point of view, a plane dealing not with a character's spoken or written words, but rather, with a character's inner thoughts or perceptions.

Again, the nonconcurrence addressed here is between dynamics on the psychological plane promoting proximity to a character, but dynamics on the informational plane promoting distance from the character. Specifically, this involves the audience being enabled to think or perceive along with a character, but doing so with an information database that possesses information lacking from the character's database.

A scene from *E.T. The Extra-Terrestrial* (1982) should make this dynamic clear. This is a movie about an extra-terrestrial being who is left behind when his spacecraft is forced to leave abruptly. E.T. is found by ten-year-old Elliot who, together with his brother Michael and sister Gertie, try to keep E.T. hidden from their mother Mary, their primary hiding place being a walk-in closet crowded with large plush toys. At one point, Mary is just about to step out the front door when she hears something upstairs. The camera catches her starting up the stairs, and then cuts to a shot from inside a bedroom closet shooting out through the slats in the closet door, capturing Mary first looking around the bedroom, then turning toward the closet and opening the doors. The camera stays on her as she looks briefly to her right, and then to her left. The camera follows her gaze by panning slowly across a collection of plush toys, taking in a raggedy-Anne doll, then a stuffed bear, then another raggedy-Anne doll, then a stuffed dog, then a stuffed lion, then *the head of E.T.* as he sits motionless among the plush toys, then simply continues past E.T. to scan the rest of the plush toys.[6]

The camera's scan across the plush toys mimics what Mary is seeing. It is essentially providing the viewers with a vantage point inside Mary's head, looking out through her eyes. This constitutes an inside view of this character, a proximity-producing device on the psychological plane of point of view. At the same time, however, the fact Mary's scan across the plush toys does not hesitate at all when it comes to E.T.'s head is a clear indication she does not recognize him for what he is. In informational-plane terms, her information database does not contain the fact that this strange-looking head belongs to an extra-terrestrial. Further, because this fact is part of the viewers' information database, a divergence is created between the databases of character and viewers, resulting in the viewers being distanced from Mary. And this combination of proximity on the psychological plane and distance on the informational plane creates dramatic irony, with the viewers being given a sense of superiority over this character.

A biblical passage reflecting these dynamics can be found in Esther 6:1–12. In the concluding verse of the preceding chapter, Haman is shown planning to have Mordecai hanged, while the opening verses of chapter 6 report how King Ahasuerus comes to decide to honor Mordecai for uncovering an assassination plot against the king. In 6:6, as a result of the king having asked Haman, "What should be done for the man whom the king desires to honor," Haman is depicted as saying in his heart, "Whom would the king desire to honor more than me?"

Because these words are spoken *in his heart*, they constitute an inside view, thus drawing the readers into a proximal position to Haman on the psychological plane of point of view. At the same time, these words reflect that Haman's information database lacks the fact the king's question is related to his intention to honor Mordecai. And because the readers' information database does contain this fact, a divergence arises between the databases of the readers and Haman, creating within the readers a sense of distance from Haman, specifically, a feeling of superiority over him.

---

6. At 45:22—45:54.

nine

A Perspective-Critical Analysis of the *Butch Cassidy* Clip

BACK IN THE FIRST chapter of this work, a seven-minute segment of the film *Butch Cassidy and the Sundance Kid* was described in minute detail. Further, it was suggested the point-of-view crafting of the scenes in this segment had the effect of leading the viewers to empathize with Butch and Sundance in their plight, and thus pull for them to be able to escape the impossible predicament in which they found themselves at the end of the segment. The specifics of that point-of-view crafting were not explained at that point, though an explanation was promised later, after there had been the opportunity to set out the various means available to storytellers for manipulating point of view. The preceding six chapters have set out those means, and so, we are now in a position to unpack the point-of-view strategy of the *Butch Cassidy* clip shot-by-shot.

Recall Butch and Sundance had already been engaged in a cat-and-mouse chase with a posse of law-enforcement officers for an eighteen-minute segment of the movie by the time we reach the series of scenes of our seven-minute segment. The first few seconds of this segment depict Butch and Sundance on a horse galloping across an area of desert conditions, mirroring numerous similar shots scattered throughout the preceding eighteen minutes of the chase. With regards to point of view on the *spatial* plane, this short shot establishes the camera in a position in proximity to Butch and Sundance. By itself, this is not significant. However, if it represents the first of a series of shots positioning the viewers in proximity to Butch and Sundance, then it is significant, for it would constitute a component of the

117

spatial-plane move of following characters, a move contributing to establishing such characters as point-of-view characters.

Next comes the scene of Butch flopping into a pool of water and cooling off, interrupted by Sundance who, peering off into the distance, indicates he has spotted something. Butch comes over alongside Sundance, and also peers off in the same direction, at which point the camera cuts to a shot of the posse in the distance. This sequence is relevant to point of view on the *psychological* plane. Having Sundance and Butch both peering off in the same direction followed immediately by a point-of-view shot—that is, a shot of what they are seeing—constitutes an inside view in that it has the effect of drawing the viewers into the heads of these characters to look out through their eyes.

While staring down at the posse, Butch makes two comments. The first is, "They're beginning to get on my nerves." This comment is also significant to point of view on the *psychological* plane. Note that when Butch speaks these words, he does not turn to address them to Sundance, who is right beside him. Rather, he speaks them while continuing to peer down at the posse, giving the impression he is saying them to no one in particular. These words do not come across as a part of a communication process with another character, but rather, come across as a verbalized expression of thought. As we saw in the section entitled "Expressions of Thought" in chapter 3, this is a cinematic device consisting of a thought of a character being turned into a verbal statement for no other reason than to allow the viewers to become aware of something happening inside the head of the character, something of which the viewers would not otherwise be aware. With this verbalized expression of thought by Butch, the viewers are treated to another inside view of this character.

The second thing Butch says here is, "Who are those guys?" This has relevance on the *informational* plane of point of view. In uttering this question, Butch makes it clear that the identities of the posse members is something not a part of his information database. Further, the viewers also have not yet been informed of the identities of the posse members either. This means there exists a convergence between the information databases of the viewers and Butch.

In response to Butch's question, Sundance prompts Butch to think back to an encounter years earlier where they became aware of a tracker who called himself Lord Baltimore, and then suggests one of the posse members down below is this Lord Baltimore. This also is significant to point of view

A Perspective-Critical Analysis of the Butch Cassidy Clip

on the *informational* plane. At the point when Butch asks, "Who are those guys?" the identities of the members of the posse were not part of their information database. However, their information database here receives a new datum, that one of the posse members is Lord Baltimore. Further, as this datum is being added to their database, it is also being added to the viewers' database, thus maintaining the convergence between the databases of the viewers and the two characters.

As Sundance abandons his vantage point to prepare to leave, Butch remains for a moment longer, still peering into the distance, with the camera then cutting to a final shot of the posse. This short sequence is relevant to point of view on the *psychological* plane, for the combination of Butch looking off into the distance followed immediately by a point-of-view shot of what Butch is seeing constitutes another inside view of Butch.

This is followed by shots of Butch and Sundance riding down a creek, and then, starting up the side of a mountain located beside the creek. Here, again, the *spatial* plane comes into play. Both the outlaws and the posse were in view in the preceding scene, and so, both are candidates to garner the attention of the camera in this following scene. However, it is again only Butch and Sundance who garner that attention, with the camera remaining in proximity to them, following them down the creek and up the base of the mountain.

The next shot comes from a camera partway up the mountain, shooting down from that position and capturing the course of the creek going off into the distance, with Butch entering the frame in the foreground, and looking back along the creek. This shot is significant to the *psychological* plane, for the fact the camera is angled to shoot in precisely the same direction Butch is looking means the viewers are given the same view Butch has. Though this is not technically an inside view—in that it is not a point-of-view shot mimicking exactly what Butch sees—it has the same function as an inside view.

As Butch looks back, he exclaims, "Damn it!" and mutters as he continues to climb, "Don't they get tired? Don't they get hungry? Why don't they slow up? Hell, they could even go faster . . . at least that would be a change!" Here, again, Butch is not saying these things to anyone in particular. Rather, these are simply more verbalized expressions of the thoughts running through this head in these circumstances, and as such, qualify as more inside views.

Perspective Criticism

This is followed by some short shots of Butch, Sundance, and the horse scrambling up the mountain; these shots continue the following of Butch and Sundance on the *spatial* plane. Then, as they stop for a rest, Butch asks Sundance whom he considers to be the best lawman, and when he answers "Joe Lefors," Butch replies, "Gotta be," pointing out he always wears a white straw hat, just as the camera cuts to the posse at a full gallop, the lead rider wearing a white hat. Here, again, the *informational* plane is in play. Before this point, Butch and Sundance were aware of the identity of only one of the six posse members, Lord Baltimore, with the identities of the other five being blanks in their information database. Likewise, the viewers had blanks in their database on the other posse members' identities, and so, there existed a convergence between the databases of the outlaws and the viewers. Then Butch has a hunch on the identity of the posse's leader, and at the same time this idea becomes implanted in the database of Butch and Sundance, it also becomes implanted in the database of the viewers. Therefore, the convergence between the databases of the outlaws and the viewers is maintained.

The camera then catches Sundance gazing into the distance, and then cuts to another shot of the posse. Because this shot is given immediately after the shot of Sundance gazing into the distance, it constitutes another point-of-view shot depicting what it is Sundance is seeing. As far as the *psychological* plane is concerned, this is another inside view of this character.

As Butch and Sundance continue their climb, the camera captures them from various angles, but all these shots are taken from positions in proximity to them; on the *spatial* plane, the camera continues to follow them. And as if to emphasize this, the camera cuts to a distance shot of the posse charging across a clearing far below, and then zooms all the way in to capture what is right in front of the camera—Butch, Sundance, and the horse struggling up the steep grade—thus conveying in another way how the camera is in proximity to Butch and Sundance, and not in proximity to the posse.

As Sundance moves past the position of the camera, it captures him looking back over his shoulder, and then immediately cuts to another distance shot of the posse. Here is yet another move on the *psychological* plane, that is, an inside view in the form of a point-of-view shot of what Sundance sees.

Butch and Sundance are then shown practically rock-climbing, having to pick their way over and around boulders as their path up the side of

A Perspective-Critical Analysis of the Butch Cassidy Clip

the mountain gets even steeper. On the *spatial* plane, the camera continues to maintain a position in proximity to Butch and Sundance as it follows these two characters.

The camera captures most of this rock-climbing from positions to the side of Butch and Sundance's path of ascent, thus showing them climb past the camera. However, as they near the top, the camera establishes a position above them, shooting down upon them. And during this shot, they are shown looking back down the mountain just as the posse ride up thirty feet below them. This is another example of a *psychological*-plane move, seen earlier. The camera is angled to shoot in the same direction Butch and Sundance are looking, thus giving the viewers the same view these two characters have. Therefore, this shot functions in the same way as an inside view, despite the fact the camera is not giving a true point-of-view shot of these characters.

The camera then captures Butch and Sundance staggering across the flat top of the mountain, then sliding down a gravelly slope on the other side, and finally finding themselves trapped on a rocky plateau one-hundred feet above a river below. With these shots, the *spatial*-plane strategy of following these two characters continues, as the camera is maintained in proximity to Butch and Sundance.[1]

At the end of the treatment of this clip from *Butch Cassidy and the Sundance Kid* back in chapter 1, the question was raised as to why the viewers found themselves pulling for these outlaws to escape from the law enforcement officers in pursuit. The answer given was "point of view," but it was not clear *how* point of view was able to accomplish that feat. Now, this should be clear. On a number of planes of point of view, moves have been designed to establish Butch and Sundance as point-of-view characters, and when the viewers experience all these events through the point of view of Butch and Sundance, they come to empathize with them, and thus, pull for them to escape.

Probably the single most powerful point-of-view move at work in this clip is the *spatial*-plane strategy of following. Despite the fact there are eight characters involved in the events depicted in these scenes, the camera is never positioned in proximity to six of them—the posse members—but always shoots them as being in the distance. Rather, the camera is always

---

1. The proximity to these two characters is actually broken right at the end of this sequence, with the camera being drawn back to a position about fifty yards away from them, but this is done only to provide the viewers with a wide enough vista to realize their predicament.

positioned in proximity to just Butch and Sundance, leading the viewers to feel as if they are experiencing the events right along with these two characters, thus contributing toward the viewers merge with Butch and Sundance.

However, as developed in chapter 8, in the section entitled "Proximity on Spatial Plane / Distance on Psychological Plane," simply following a character for even a lengthy stretch of a narrative may not succeed in establishing him or her as a point-of-view character. The camera may be positioned in proximity to a character continuously, but if nothing of the character's inner life is revealed—nothing in the way of thoughts or emotions or motivations—he or she will simply come across as an enigma. Therefore, in our look at Butch and Sundance, it is necessary to go beyond just the spatial plane to examine the *psychological* plane as well.

Our shot-by-shot analysis has revealed ample psychological-plane data. On two occasions, Butch is shown giving verbalized expressions of thought, and these constitute inside views. And as we saw back in chapter 3, being provided with such views into the inner life of a character leads the viewers to take up a vantage point inside the head of the character. Further, such a vantage point results in the viewers experiencing the events of the story world as if they are looking out through the character's eyes, and this makes a strong contribution toward the viewers coming to merge with the character.

Inside views of Butch and Sundance also occur by means of multiple instances of point-of-view shots, where the viewers are actually positioned inside the characters' heads to look out through their eye sockets at what they are seeing. In addition, there are two cases of what might be called "*pseudo* point-of-view shots"—that is, shots in which the camera is shooting in the same direction a character is looking, thus giving the viewers the view the character has, but also capturing the character as well—and these also have the effect of inside views. Therefore, the viewers are continually taken inside the heads of Butch and Sundance, and this supplements the effect of continuously following these characters.

Activity on the *informational* plane of point of view also makes a contribution toward establishing Butch and Sundance as point-of-view characters. At the beginning of this sequence of scenes, Butch and Sundance know they are being chased by a six-man posse, but they are not aware of the identities of any of its members. Likewise, the viewers are not aware of any of their identities either, this information having been withheld from them.

A Perspective-Critical Analysis of the Butch Cassidy Clip

Therefore, a convergence between the information database of Butch and Sundance and the information database of the viewers exists at the outset.

During the course of the events covered in this sequence of scenes, Butch and Sundance begin to figure out the identities of some of the posse's members, and as each of their identities came to light to Butch and Sundance, the viewers also become aware of them. Therefore, the convergence between the information databases of the characters and the viewers is maintained, with each new piece of information being added to the viewers' database only as it is being added to the characters' database. And this informational-plane dynamic contributes further to the viewers coming to merge with Butch and Sundance, and thus empathizing with them in the predicament they face at the end of the sequence of scenes.

With the basic storyline of this sequence—six law enforcement officers pursuing two outlaws—it is obviously not necessary to present the story in such a way as to have the viewers side with the outlaws to escape from the law enforcement officers. With this fact pattern, it would have been just as easy to craft the story such that the viewers are siding with the law enforcement officers to catch the outlaws. Following is a retelling of the exact same events, but in a way the viewers' sentiments are with the posse, and especially Joe Lefors, as opposed to with Butch and Sundance:

> The posse crested a hill, and before them was land stripped of dirt, leaving a solid rock surface. Lefors dropped from his horse at the lead position of the posse and stared out over the rocky expanse. "How can we possibly maintain the scent over solid rock?" he thought to himself. While deep in thought, he felt a hand on his shoulder. He turned to see Lord Baltimore standing next to him, with a look that appeared to be intended to convey reassurance. "Don't worry," he said. "Remember, I can track anyone, anywhere, over any type of terrain . . . even this rock." He immediately began scanning the ground in search of clues. Lefors remounted his horse, muttering to himself, "If anyone's gonna be able to track them bandits, it's the Indian."
>
> The Indian led the posse slowly across the rock, finally making it to terrain more conducive to tracking. He quickly picked up the bandits' trail, pointing out their route to the others. Lefors felt a big sense of relief as the six of them took off in that direction. While riding along the edge of a gully, Lefors noticed dust being kicked up a far way off, on the other side of the gully. He looked closer, and saw it was a horse with two riders. The bandits were finally in

> sight! He pointed out the find to the others, and they all increased their pace to a gallop.
>
> Lefors saw the bandits starting up the side of a mountain. Vegetation on the mountain was sparse, so Lefors was able to track the bandits' route of ascent. As he himself reached the beginning of the ascent, he saw that the bandits had dismounted. "The incline must be getting too steep for their horse to keep climbing with the two riders," Lefors surmised. "This is where we really make up ground, boys," he shouted to the others, knowing that their horses had been trained to handle the steeper grade with ease . . .

This telling of the events is intended to have the readers empathize with the posse, as opposed to with Butch and Sundance, and the means for accomplishing this is simply point-of-view moves designed to establish Joe Lefors as the point-of-view character. This account will now undergo the same type of perspective-critical analysis afforded the original movie clip, isolating these point-of-view moves and expounding upon their effect.

The account opens with the posse coming to the rocky expanse, Lefors dismounting and surveying the sight. With regards to the *spatial* plane of point of view, the camera positioning here is the opposite of that used in the original movie clip. As opposed to being positioned in proximity to Butch and Sundance, the camera is positioned in proximity to the posse members. The focus is clearly on Lefors, as he is isolated from the other members of the posse. However, this is not to say he is necessarily being established as the point-of-view character to the exclusion of the others, for singling out a particular character like this could simply be for the purpose of giving a focused *external* view of him, which actually works *against* that character being established as the point-of-view character. Rather, establishment as a point-of-view character always requires at least some *subjective* experience of him or her, by means of something like inside views into what is happening in the character's inner life.

The following report of him wondering how they will possibly be able to track Butch and Sundance over rock constitutes just such an inside view. This *psychological*-plane move does indeed suggest he might be established as the point-of-view character, as opposed to the whole posse being established as a point-of-view group character.

The following couple of sentences contain more inside views that solidify Lefors in this role. The first of these sentences describes how he *feels* a hand on his shoulder. While other characters may be able to see the hand being placed on his shoulder, only Lefors' brain is registering the pressure of a hand being laid on his shoulder. Therefore, just like reports of what a character *sees* or *hears* communicate to the readers what is registering in the character's brain—thus qualifying as inside views—so also this report of what Lefors *feels* qualifies as an inside view.

The next sentence depicts Lefors turning and seeing Lord Baltimore, and then continues "with a look that appeared to be intended to convey reassurance." First, the reference to Lefors turning to "see" Lord Baltimore is an inside view, transporting the readers inside his head to look out his eye sockets at Lord Baltimore standing there. Further, though the quoted section of the sentence does not fit the definition of inside view developed to this point, it does actually constitute one. Note how these words reference a look that *appears* to be intended to convey reassurance. This does not reflect the point of view of the narrator who, being omniscient, is fully aware of the intention behind the look, and so, would not speak in terms of just what the look *appears* to convey. Rather, this reflects the point of view of Lefors; it is in his mind that the look *appears* to be intended to convey reassurance. Therefore, we have another inside view of this character.

The concluding statement of the paragraph—that Lefors remounts his horse and mutters to himself, "If anyone's gonna be able to track them bandits, it's the Indian"—is significant on the *phraseological* plane of point of view. Note how he uses the term "bandits" to refer to Butch and Sundance, and the term "the Indian" when referring to Lord Baltimore. Assuming Lefors has used these terms repeatedly in reference to these characters to this point in the storyline, they would now constitute phraseological traits of Lefors. This being the case, instances later in the narrative of their usage *in narratorial speech* would function to signal the narrator is adopting Lefors' point of view on the phraseological plane, thus contributing toward establishing him as a point-of-view character.

At the beginning of the next paragraph, the *phraseological* plane of point of view already comes into play. In the first sentence, the narrator says, "*The Indian* led the posse slowly across the rock . . ." The narrator's own phraseological trait for referring to this character is "Lord Baltimore," and so, under ordinary circumstances, the narrator would have simply said here, "*Lord Baltimore* led the posse slowly across the rock . . ." The fact the narrator substitutes "the Indian" for "Lord Baltimore" signals the narrator is adopting Lefors' point of view on the phraseological plane.

In the following sentence, the narrator says, "He quickly picked up *the bandits*' trail . . ." The narrator has established "Butch and Sundance" as his phraseological trait for referring to these two characters. However, he here foregoes that in favor of inserting "the bandits" here. By doing so, he adopts Lefors' phraseological trait for referring to Butch and Sundance, thus continuing to solidify Lefors' status as a point-of-view character.

The following sentences reveal more moves on the *psychological* plane. First, there is mention that Lefors "felt" a big sense of relief, an inside view of Lefors. The next sentence presents another inside view, in mentioning that Lefors "noticed" dust being kicked up in the distance. The following sentence reveals yet another. It is not the reference that Lefors "*looked*"; as mentioned in the "Expressions of Seeing" section of chapter 3, the act of looking does not qualify as an inside view. However, the following mention that Lefors "saw" a horse with two riders does provide an indication of something registering in Lefors' brain, and therefore, constitutes a third inside view. There is clearly a strong push on the psychological plane to have the readers merge with Lefors.

In this paragraph, the posse members are no longer the only characters in the scene, as Butch and Sundance join them. With the presence of these two character groups, the narrator now has a choice of positions in which to place the readers: in proximity to the posse members or in proximity to Butch and Sundance. Faced with this choice, the narrator continues to follow the posse members, and specifically, Lefors, with Butch and Sundance appearing only in the distance. On the *spatial plane*, the readers continue to be led to experience these events through the point of view of Lefors.

The final paragraph begins with the readers continuing to be placed in a *spatial* position in proximity to Lefors. Further, the reference to Butch and Sundance as "the bandits" constitutes another *phraseological*-plane move, with the narrator again adopting a phraseological trait of Lefors into narratorial speech. However, movements on the *psychological* plane dominate the point-of-view crafting here.

In the first sentence, there is mention that Lefors "saw" the bandits starting up the mountain, and the third sentence also includes a reference that he "saw" the bandits had dismounted their horse; these inside views place the readers inside Lefors' head to look out through his eyes at Butch and Sundance. Further, the fourth sentence consists of a *thought* of Lefors regarding the capabilities of the bandits' horse, another inside view that takes the readers into the head of Lefors. Finally, the fifth sentence concludes with a piece of *reasoning* behind Lefors' statement to the other posse

A Perspective-Critical Analysis of the Butch Cassidy Clip

members—that their making up ground on the bandits is assured due to the superior conditioning of their horses—another inside view of Lefors.

To summarize, this new account of the events utilizes point-of-view moves on a number of planes to create within the readers a sense of empathy for Joe Lefors, as opposed to the sense of empathy for Butch and Sundance evident in the movie clip. On the spatial plane, the narrator keeps the readers in proximity to Lefors, with Butch and Sundance only appearing far off in the distance. On the psychological plane, the readers are given several inside views of Lefors. On the phraseological plane, the narrator inserts two phraseological traits of Lefors into narratorial speech. Together, these point-of-view moves lead the readers to view these events through the point of view of Lefors, resulting in the readers empathizing with him, and thus, pulling for him to succeed in preventing Butch and Sundance from escaping.

In this chapter, we started with the analysis of certain point-of-view moves in the *Butch Cassidy* clip that lead the audience to empathize with Butch and Sundance, and thus, pull for them to escape the posse. Then we looked at the same events reported using different point-of-view moves, and we found ourselves empathizing with Joe Lefors, and thus, pulling for him to catch Butch and Sundance. What we have seen here is the *power* of point of view in action. In the final two chapters, we apply the same kind of analysis to narrative texts from the Bible.

ten

New Testament Case Study
Gamaliel (Acts 5:35–39)

IN ACTS 5, THE apostles are arrested and brought before the Sanhedrin for a second time, and even go so far as to provoke the members of the Sanhedrin to the point that they want them put to death. Into this powder keg of a situation steps Gamaliel to suggest the council not put them to death, but rather, simply wait and see. He reasons that if these men's actions are not of God, they will fail, but if their actions are of God, they will succeed, and efforts in opposition to them would constitute fighting against God (vv. 35–39).

In this passage, the Lukan narrator does not provide explicit evaluative guidance as to whether the readers are to view this advice of Gamaliel in a favorable light or in an unfavorable light. Some biblical interpreters have argued that the principle Gamaliel presents here is intended as a model for how the church should act when faced with something new. Other interpreters have seen Gamaliel's principle as intended to be taken as ironic in that Gamaliel's thinking behind these words is that these followers of Jesus are going to fail, whereas the readers know these followers of Jesus continue to bear witness even to the ends of the earth.

William John Lyons' treatment of this issue presents detailed summaries of two works, one on each side of the debate,[1] and his treatment is especially interesting for our purposes since both of the works he covers utilize a *narrative* approach to the issue. Lyons summarizes works by

---

1. Lyons, "Words of Gamaliel," 23–49.

New Testament Case Study

David Gowler and John Darr on this issue,[2] pointing out they both base their analyses on the characterization of the Pharisees. According to Lyons, the main reason the two scholars come to opposing conclusions on Gamaliel—Gowler judging him positively and Darr negatively—is their differing stances on the issue of the relation between Luke and Acts. Darr sees them as two parts of the same narrative with the negative characterization of the Pharisees in Luke contributing toward an equally negative characterization of them in Acts. Gowler, on the other hand, considers them as two separate narratives, and believes the assessment of the Pharisees in Acts is actually quite positive when not influenced by the negative characterization of them in Luke.

To rely on the analysis of characterization to determine whether Gamaliel is intended to be viewed positively or negatively is problematic. This approach inevitably involves collecting data on a character from throughout a narrative to form a comprehensive portrait of the character, with the determination of whether a particular act by the character is intended to be met with approval or disapproval depending on whether the character's portrait is positive or negative.

An approach like this presupposes the possibility of forming an all-encompassing character grid which, when set over any action performed by that character, is able to provide a clear indication of how the readers are to assess the action. However, it is highly questionable whether such a grid could ever be produced. If a story were populated only with simple characters who always acted with total consistency, grids of this type could be produced. However, most of the stories of the Bible do not fit this description, for they have characters who are complex, who defy being fit into static grids.

The use of the word "static" here is intentional, for it points out the problem. The conventional approach to characterization studies is static in nature, in that it presupposes a story is an object existing in space. Conceiving of a story in this way allows the interpreter to see all parts of the story at the same time, and this leads to interpreters feeling free to draw data from all parts of the story as they assemble still-shot portraits of characters. However, a story is not an object existing in space, but rather, an event existing in time. As such, it is dynamic in nature with story elements progressing, developing, evolving. This being the case, it is virtually impossible to produce a still-shot portrait of a character, for he or she will not

---

2. Gowler, *Host*; Darr, *Character Building*.

necessarily be the same from one section of the story to the next, and might even be the total opposite.

More importantly for our purposes, the fact characters can change throughout the course of a narrative means a narrator may want the readers to approve of a character's actions at one point in the storyline, but disapprove of his or her actions at another point. For narratives such as these, a still-shot portrait of a character is incapable of indicating which actions should be met with approval, and which should be met with disapproval.

On the other hand, the methodology of point-of-view analysis developed in the present work is able to do so. Because it does not rely on data accumulated throughout a whole narrative, but rather, relies only on the data attached to the particular passage under examination, it has the capacity of making individual assessments of each act committed by a character. Therefore, even if the overall characterization of a character is overwhelmingly positive, this methodology is able to isolate even a single act that is intended by the narrator to be met with the readers' disapproval, and vice versa.

This chapter will be devoted to a demonstration of how a perspective-critical analysis can make a contribution to the issue of whether Gamaliel's advice is intended to be viewed favorably or unfavorably by the readers. The point-of-view crafting of Acts 5 will be examined, starting at a point prior to the actual appearance of Gamaliel in verse 34, for the readers' positioning going into the material covering Gamaliel will influence whether or not the readers perceive this character as the point-of-view character of the passage.

As we embark on an analysis of the workings of point of view on the various planes of this narrative text, it is expedient to note here at the outset that the *temporal* plane need not be considered. As we saw back in chapter 5, there exist only a few temporal-plane dynamics capable of making a contribution to the process of establishing a particular character as a point-of-view character, and none of them are in play in this passage. However, data from the other planes of point of view are more than ample for coming to a determination on whether the readers are here being led to merge with Gamaliel.

As background to our passage, the apostles' preaching has come to the attention of the Sanhedrin who order them to cease speaking in the name of Jesus (4:1–18), but Peter and John refuse to relent, claiming they are not able to cease proclaiming what they have seen and heard (4:19–20). Their continued ministry has a significant impact on the people of Jerusalem (5:12–16), leading to the reaction of the Jewish religious leaders seen in our passage.

Verses 17–18 report jealousy of the apostles on the part of the high priest and his associates—a group character encompassing these two parties, as well as others, hereafter referred to as the "religious leaders"—which results in the apostles being arrested. An analysis of the *spatial* plane of point of view in these verses reveals evidence suggesting the readers are being placed in a position closer to the religious leaders than to the apostles. Recall from the discussion of Kuno's Syntactic Prominence Principle back in the "Linguistics Affecting Readers' Distance From Characters" section of chapter 2, readers are most inclined to empathize with the element of a clause possessing the most syntactic prominence, that is, the one closest to the head of the clause, and thus, encountered by the readers first. As between the religious leaders and the apostles, it is the former whom the readers encounter first while proceeding through these verses. Indeed, the apostles are not mentioned at all in verse 17—despite the fact they are clearly the target of the religious leaders' jealousy mentioned in this verse—thus leaving the religious leaders as the sole focus of attention at the outset. With this juxtaposition of these two group characters, it is as though the camera begins with a shot of the religious leaders alone, and only subsequently pans to one side to capture the apostles. This establishes the religious leaders as a vantage point from which the subsequent shot of the apostles is taken, resulting in the readers viewing the apostles through the point of view of the religious leaders.

These verses also include a detail relevant to point of view on the *psychological* plane. At the end of verse 17, it is mentioned that the religious leaders are "filled with jealousy," thus providing the readers with an inside view into the emotions of this group character. This subjective experience of the inner workings of the religious leaders has the potential of contributing toward drawing the readers into proximity to them.

However, our discussion of inside views back in the "Special Considerations in Analyzing Inside Views" section of chapter 3 made it clear a single inside view does not, by itself, bring readers into a position of proximity with the character whose inner life is being laid bare. It is possible the inside view in verse 17 is the beginning of a cluster extending into the material in the following verses, and so, our assessment of the workings of point of view on the psychological plane in the opening of this passage will need to wait until we have had a chance to examine this later material.

Regarding the workings of point of view on the *informational* plane of verses 17–18, the fact the religious leaders experience jealousy toward the apostles and have them arrested is information to which both the leaders and the readers are privy, and so, the information databases of readers and leaders converge here. On the other hand, because the apostles are not aware of the fact the religious leaders are jealous of them, but the readers are aware of this fact, there is a divergence between the databases of the readers and apostles to begin the passage. However, the following fact that the apostles are arrested and put into jail is information to which both the readers and apostles are privy, and so, the initial divergence between their databases is transformed into a convergence.

Verses 19–21*a* report how an angel releases the apostles from the prison and instructs them to continue teaching the people, and how the apostles comply. This marks a change on the *spatial* plane, as the readers are taken from a position in proximity to the religious leaders established in verses 17–18, and are placed in a position of proximity to the apostles.[3]

The fact that the religious leaders disappear from the scene impacts the *informational* plane of point of view, for the convergence between the information databases of the religious leaders and the readers forming in verses 17–18 now turns into a divergence, as all the information regarding the angel's visit and the apostles' reaction is added to the readers' database, but not to the religious leaders' database. Further, the convergence between the databases of the apostles and the readers which began in verse 18 continues to strengthen in these new verses, as the details of all the events being reported here are added to both of their databases.

In verses 21*b*–24, the religious leaders gather, and they send for the prisoners, but the attendants who are sent cannot find them in the prison and come back to report this, resulting in the captain of the temple guard and the chief priests being perplexed. Here, another shift occurs on the *spatial plane*, with the camera abandoning the apostles in favor of a position in proximity to the religious leaders—this group character encompassing the attendants, the captain of the temple guard, and the chief priests.

---

3. Technically, the readers are also placed in a position in proximity to the angel as well. However, the primary issue in the analysis of this passage is whether the readers are drawn into a position of proximity to the apostles or to the religious leaders, and so, dynamics related to secondary characters such as this angel will not be considered.

New Testament Case Study

The fact the camera has abandoned the apostles in these verses has an impact on the *informational* plane of point of view, for it means the convergence of the information databases of the readers and the apostles during verses 18–21a here turns into a divergence, since the apostles' database is not receiving any of the information being added here to the readers' database on the activities among the religious leaders. Analysis of the relation between the databases of the readers and the religious leaders is more complex. With verse 21b, there is a move from divergence toward convergence, as both readers and leaders are aware of the leaders' gathering and their sending for the prisoners. On the other hand, a point of divergence persists, for the readers are aware of a fact of which the religious leaders are not aware—that the apostles are currently in the temple—and this point of divergence continues right through verse 24. Therefore, the readers' database diverges from the databases of both the apostles and the religious leaders at this point in the passage.

Verses 25–26 report an unidentified character announcing the discovery of the prisoners in the temple, which prompts their being re-arrested. On the *spatial* plane, the camera remains in proximity to the religious leaders, specifically, to the members of the Sanhedrin as they receive the announcement of the discovery, and to the captain and the attendants of the Sanhedrin as they make the re-arrest.

The announcement in verse 25 that the prisoners are in the temple makes an impact on the *informational* plane of point of view. Up to this point, a divergence has existed between the information databases of the readers and the religious leaders in that the readers have been aware of the location of the apostles, but the religious leaders have not been. However, with this report to the religious leaders that the prisoners are in the temple, that divergence is transformed into a convergence, with the information level of the religious leaders catching up to that of the readers. Further, this convergence continues through the report in verse 26 that the captain and attendants re-arrest the apostles, for the information being added here to the readers' database is also a part of the religious leaders' database.

What of the relation between the information databases of the readers and the apostles? Since verse 21b, there has existed a divergence between the databases of the readers and the apostles, with the readers being privy to all the actions reported in verses 21b–25, but the apostles not being privy to them, since they have not been present for any of them. In verse 26, the apostles reappear, and because they are now again involved, it would seem they would be privy to the same information to which the readers are privy, resulting in a re-establishment of the earlier convergence between the databases of the readers and the apostles. However a closer look at this verse reveals the databases of the readers and the apostles remain diverged.

Note the mention of how the captain and attendants are afraid of being stoned by the people as they bring the apostles to the Sanhedrin. There is nothing in this verse indicating the apostles are aware of the fact the captain and attendants are experiencing this emotion, and since the readers are aware of this fact, there exists a divergence between the databases of the readers and the apostles.

The mention of the fear being experienced by the captain and attendants is also significant to point of view on the *psychological* plane. Because the mention reveals to the readers an emotion the captain and attendants are experiencing, it constitutes an inside view of them. Does this inside view together with the earlier one in verse 17 constitute a cluster, thus contributing to the readers feeling a sense of proximity to the religious leaders? Crucial in addressing this question is the fact that between these two inside views of the religious leaders, this character group completely disappears from the storyline (verses 19–21a), meaning the two inside views occur in two separate manifestations of the religious leaders, thus eliminating the possibility of these two inside views being considered members of the same cluster.

It is important to note that it is the inner lives of *minor* members of the "religious leaders" group character being revealed here. This is significant because the point-of-view crafting of verses 25–26 appears to be making a distinction between the minor and major members of this group character. Specifically, the point-of-view moves in these verses have the effect of de-emphasizing the sense of proximity to the minor members of this character group. These verses depict the captain and attendants—all minor members—going to re-arrest the apostles, but the point-of-view dynamics here differ from those in the report in verse 22 of the attendants not finding the apostles in the prison. There, the camera clearly moves with the attendants as they go to the prison, and follows them back after they discover the apostles are missing. Compare that with how verse 26 is crafted: "Then, the captain with the attendants having gone away, they brought them . . ." In contrast to the crafting of verse 22 which clearly involves the camera moving to the prison and back, the crafting here does not involve any movement of the camera at all; rather, it gives the impression the camera is positioned

New Testament Case Study

in proximity to the members of the Sanhedrin—major religious leaders—simply catching the captain and attendants leaving, and then catching them again when they reappear with the prisoners. Therefore, unlike verse 22 where the camera stays in proximity to the minor attendants, the report in verse 25 has the camera stay in proximity to the major Sanhedrin members. This move appears to separate the Sanhedrin members as the only significant religious leaders for the purposes of the climax of this passage.

Verses 27–32 report how the apostles are brought before the Sanhedrin and questioned on their violation of the council's order not to teach in the name of Jesus, and how the apostles declare they must obey God rather than humans. As far as the *spatial* plane of point of view is concerned, these verses are significant in that they represent the first time in the passage both the apostles and the Sanhedrin members are present at the same time. This means the narrator has a decision to make. Does he place the readers in a position in proximity to the apostles, or a position in proximity to the religious leaders, or a position equidistant from the two? If our assessment of the point-of-view dynamics of verse 26 is correct—that the narrator is there drawing the readers into proximity to the *Sanhedrin* members—it would be logical here for the narrator to place the readers in a position closer to the Sanhedrin members than to the apostles. And an analysis of the spatial plane in these verses reveals that is precisely what the narrator does.

This segment of the passage consists of an exchange between the Sanhedrin members and the apostles. The focus is first placed on the high priest as he is shown accusing the apostles of violating the Sanhedrin's order to cease teaching in the name of Jesus, and of determining to place the blame for his death upon them. The focus then shifts to Peter and the rest of the apostles for their assertion they must obey God rather than humans. What is the spatial-plane effect of this shift in focus?

Think back to Kuno's Syntactic Prominence Principle. In unpacking this principle—that more empathy is given to the character the readers encounter first—the dynamic involved was likened to a movie scene where the camera first focuses on one character, but then pans to one side to reveal another, leading the viewers to perceive the second character through the point of view of the first. In this passage, the camera would first be on the high priest—a member of the Sanhedrin—only then panning over to the apostles. The readers, then, are being led to perceive the apostles through the point of view of the Sanhedrin members. Therefore, the spatial-plane dynamics of these verses do indeed keep the readers in proximity to the religious leaders over against the apostles.

Verses 33–34 cover how the apostles' words spark fury among the members of the Sanhedrin, along with a desire to put them to death, and how this prompts Gamaliel to rise among them and order that the apostles be removed. Regarding the *spatial plane* of point of view, both the religious leaders and the apostles are present here, but the readers are clearly being placed closer to the former than the latter. First, applying Kuno's Syntactic Prominence Principle, it is the religious leaders whom the readers encounter first, as the subjects of the participle "hearing" at the beginning of verse 33, and also, as the subjects of the verbs "were infuriated" and "wanted (to kill)" that follow, all before the apostles are referenced with a mere personal pronoun at the end of the verse. Further, recall Kuno's Surface Structure Empathy Hierarchy, which stipulates that empathy is felt most easily for the *subject* of a clause, and in these verses, it is the religious leaders who are the subjects of both the participles and all three of the finite verbs. On this basis as well, the readers are being drawn into proximity to *the religious leaders*, thus continuing the spatial-plane dynamics evident in the preceding verses.

Moves on the *psychological* plane of point of view supplement these dynamics on the spatial plane. Verse 33 contains two inside views of the members of the Sanhedrin. The first is the reference to their *being infuriated* at what the apostles have said, thus providing the readers with a look into their emotional state. The second is a reference to their *wishing to do away with them*, a look into the Sanhedrin members' inner lives at a *desire* they have. Therefore, we have here a compound inside view, and this contributes further to the readers being drawn into proximity to this group character.

These two inside views also influence the dynamics of the *informational* plane. On the one hand, the facts that the members of the Sanhedrin experience infuriation and that they have the desire to have the apostles executed are being added to the readers' informational database, resulting in a convergence between the databases of the readers and the Sanhedrin members. At the same time, the readers' database here diverges from that of the apostles, for the details presented in verse 33 exhibit no clear evidence the apostles would necessarily have as a part of their information database an awareness of the Sanhedrin members' desire to have them put to death, a fact that is part of the readers' database. Therefore, dynamics on the informational plane work together with dynamics on the spatial and

New Testament Case Study

psychological planes to place the readers in a position of proximity to the religious leaders, and at a distance from the apostles.

Our analysis has now brought us to Gamaliel's speech, and the question before us is, "Does the point-of-view crafting of the material just covered influence our evaluation of what Gamaliel is about to say?" We will now review our perspective-critical findings to see if a pattern of point-of-view crafting emerges leading to the conclusion the readers are being led either to approve or disapprove of the advice Gamaliel gives in his following speech.

The passage begins with the report of the religious leaders being jealous of the apostles and having them arrested, which draws the readers into a position of proximity to the leaders on the spatial and informational planes, with an inside view of the leaders constituting a potential psychological-plane contribution toward the same end. At the same time, there is an informational-plane contribution at the end of this segment of the passage contributing towards the readers being drawn into proximity to the apostles.

The report in verses 19–21a of the apostles' release from prison and their continuing to teach the people maintains the readers in a position of proximity to the apostles on the informational plane, which is enhanced by dynamics on the spatial plane. Further, there are no additional inside views of the religious leaders to join the one in the preceding verses, leaving the readers at a distance from them on the psychological plane.

In verses 21b–24, the religious leaders are shown sending for the apostles, but the apostles are not found in the prison, resulting in perplexity among the religious leaders. The readers' proximity to the apostles in the preceding verses comes to an abrupt halt as a result of the dynamics on the spatial plane, where proximity to the religious leaders is re-established. The dynamics on the informational plane also pull the readers away from the apostles, yet do not lead them totally into proximity to the leaders, as a point of divergence is left lingering between the databases of the readers and the leaders.

This is followed in verses 25–26 by someone letting the religious leaders know the apostles are in the temple, leading to the apostles being apprehended. Here, proximity to the religious leaders is maintained on both the spatial plane and the informational plane, with dynamics on the informational plane also serving to distance the readers from the apostles.

Verses 27–32 report that the apostles are brought before the Sanhedrin to face questioning by the high priest, and also present a defense they make. The narrator's crafting of the exchange reported in these verses indicates the spatial plane is being used to maintain the readers in a position of proximity to the members of the Sanhedrin.

In verses 33–34, the Sanhedrin members are shown responding to the apostles with fury, prompting Gamaliel to order the apostles removed from their presence. Again, dynamics on the spatial plane and the informational plane serve to maintain the readers in a position of proximity to the leaders. In addition, two more inside views of the leaders make a strong contribution toward the same end on the psychological plane.

This summary reveals that the first part of the passage (vv. 17–24) exhibits no clear point-of-view strategy leading the readers in one direction or the other. Stretches of text like this are not uncommon, for the empathy producing capabilities of point-of-view crafting are not always needed, and at times when they are not needed, displays of intricate point-of-view crafting are not to be expected. A look at the content of these verses suggests this is one such time. On the one hand, empathy for the Sanhedrin members would not be expected, for they are working against the plan of God in attempting to silence the apostles. On the other hand, the only thing the apostles do in this section of the passage that is of note is resume their teaching in the temple in obedience to the angel's instructions, and that, by itself, is too minor a point to warrant the narrator's making a special effort to have the readers empathize with them in their efforts.

The rest of the passage (vv. 25–34) exhibits an entirely different point-of-view strategy. In this material, the narrator works consistently on the spatial, informational, and psychological planes to draw the readers into a position in proximity to the *members of the Sanhedrin*. In fact, the narrator even goes so far as to craft the speech of the apostles in such a way that it does not pull the readers away from the religious leaders.

At first glance, this appears to be a strange strategy to employ, for according to what we have seen with regards to point-of-view and empathy dynamics, this strategy is apparently designed to have the readers approve of the Sanhedrin members' actions reported here. Obviously, the narrator cannot be trying to draw the readers into approving of the high priest's chastisement of the apostles, or the Sanhedrin's fury at the apostles' assertion that they must obey the command of God rather than the orders of humans. So, what could explain the narrator drawing the readers into a position of proximity to the members of the Sanhedrin here?

This move gives the readers the sense of being positioned right in the midst of the Sanhedrin. This being the case, when verse 34 reports Gamaliel rising up to order that the apostles be removed, the readers would sense he is arising *right at their side*. Therefore, the proximity the narrator has spent ten verses building has not been for the purpose of having the readers be close to the religious leaders as a whole, or even to the Sanhedrin members as a whole. Rather, it has been for the purpose of having the readers reach verse 34 in a position *in proximity to Gamaliel in particular* when he arises out of the midst of his colleagues to address them. And this sense of proximity to Gamaliel functions to engender within the readers a feeling of empathy for him, and thus, incline them to *approve* of what he says.

In essence, what we have here is parallel to the situation faced by Jane Austen in her writing of *Emma*, as outlined back in chapter 1. Austen had a character who, because of her proclivity for meddling, is an unsympathetic character, and the Lukan narrator has a character who, being a Pharisee and a member of the Sanhedrin, is also an unsympathetic character. Further, Austen wants her readers to empathize with Emma despite her misdeeds, and for leading readers to empathize with unsympathetic characters, establishing them as point-of-view characters is the most effective—indeed, the *only*—means for accomplishing the task. And it appears the Lukan narrator has also employed this narrative dynamic to accomplish the same task.

eleven

Old Testament Case Study
Gideon (Judges 6:36–40)

HERE, IN THE FINAL chapter of this work, we come full circle back to the biblical scenario that opened the book: the account of Gideon twice requesting a sign from God through the laying out of a fleece overnight (Judg 6:36–40). When this account was brought up in chapter 1, it was pointed out that this story of Gideon does not include any explicit, evaluative guidance leading the readers to applaud or condemn the actions of Gideon. Therefore, the question remains whether what Gideon does here is intended as a model for discerning God's will, or merely as a blatant demonstration of a lack of faith on his part.

In a 1997 article, Daniel I. Block points out that the portrayal of Gideon in Judges 6–9 has given rise to two opposing views on him. On the one hand, there is what he calls the Traditional Pious Response: "Although the narrative hints at flaws in Gideon's character, on the whole he must be evaluated positively,"[1] and Block is able to enumerate twenty points in support of this position. On the other hand, a Holistic Literary Response believes that "this idealized picture can be maintained only by disregarding an impressive list of contrary data,"[2] which he proceeds to present in the form of sixteen negative observations on Gideon.

While Block's work stands as a helpful compendium of points making up the characterization of Gideon in the book of Judges, it is the position of the present work that the mere tabulation of positive or negative

---

1. Block, "Real Gideon," 356.
2. Ibid., 359.

Old Testament Case Study

observations is not sufficient, in itself, for making an adjudication on whether *a particular action* of a character is to be evaluated positively or negatively. Is it not possible that a character who has been consistently evaluated positively in a narrative might commit a deed regarding which the narrator intends the readers to disapprove? Likewise, could not a negatively characterized character perform an action worthy of approval? There is no accounting for situations like these when the interpreter relies simply on characterization data.

Perspective criticism, on the other hand, possesses the capacity to discern a narrator's evaluation of a character in a particular passage *using nothing but the data in the passage itself*. And being unhindered by how the character has been characterized elsewhere in the narrative, a perspective-critical analysis could very well uncover an evaluation of a character not in keeping with the general characterization of him or her in the narrative. One need only analyze the point-of-view crafting of the passage itself to see whether it leads the readers to merge with the character (in which case approval is intended) or to be distanced from the character (and thus disapprove of the character's actions).

We shall now conduct a perspective-critical analysis of Gideon and the fleece to see if an examination of the point-of-view crafting of this passage reveals any patterns related to either drawing the readers into a position of proximity to Gideon or holding the readers back in a position at a distance from him. However, we will not be examining just the five verses covering the actual fleece incident. Rather, we will also be covering the material leading up to these five verses, for point-of-view moves in these preceding verses may have a bearing on how the point-of-view moves in the actual passage are to be interpreted.

The passage opens with a report in verses 11–12a of the meeting of Gideon and the angel of the Lord. With regards to point of view on the *spatial* plane, the narrator initially positions the readers in proximity to the angel, and only then is Gideon introduced with a mention of him beating out wheat somewhere at a distance from this initial position, with the angel—and the readers—moving toward Gideon's position in verse 12a to facilitate the meeting.

Verses 12b–18 relate an interaction between the angel and Gideon, as the angel attempts to commission Gideon to deliver Israel out of the hands of the Midianites, but meets with reluctance on Gideon's part. Regarding the *spatial* plane of point of view, the readers have now moved with the angel into the presence of Gideon, resulting in their being equidistant from the angel and Gideon.

On the *informational* plane, the readers are here distanced from Gideon by virtue of his failure to recognize the visitor is Yahweh.[3] The readers' information database receives the detail the visitor is Yahweh right at the beginning of the passage (v. 11), and this point is reinforced in verses 12, 14, and 16. On the other hand, this key detail is kept from Gideon's information database not only when he first meets the visitor, but all the way through their initial interaction. As a result, there is a divergence between the databases of the readers and Gideon, and this creates within the readers a sense of distance from Gideon, as the readers experience this interaction with a totally different perspective than that possessed by Gideon.

Verse 19 reports Gideon going away, preparing food, and bringing it back for his visitor, and the point-of-view dynamics of this verse represent a marked difference from those of the preceding verses. First, the *spatial* positioning changes here. Unlike the preceding verses which had the readers in the presence of both the angel and Gideon, verse 19 rips the readers away from the angel and places them only in proximity to Gideon. In addition, syntactic-prominence dynamics are different here. As developed back in chapter 2, in the section entitled "Linguistics Affecting Readers' Distance From Characters," word order in biblical Hebrew will generally have the verb first, followed by the subject, and this is indeed the pattern we see throughout the interaction between Gideon and the angel presented in verses 12b–18. However, verse 19 brings about a break in this pattern by placing the subject Gideon before the verb, in the position of maximum syntactic prominence, and this ascribing of syntactic prominence to Gideon also contributes toward the readers being brought into proximity to Gideon on the spatial plane.

However, at the same time spatial-plane moves are functioning to bring the readers into proximity to Gideon, the dynamics on the *informational* plane continue to hold the readers back from him. As we have seen, the readers' information database contains the fact the visitor is the angel of Yahweh, but Gideon's information database still does not contain this piece of information; the divergence between the two databases continues.

---

3. Soggin, *Judges*, 114, explains that "the angel of Yahweh" is not used to designate an angel with autonomous existence as reflected in late Judaism, but rather, simply to designate the visible manifestation of Yahweh.

Old Testament Case Study

A move on the *temporal* plane of verse 19 also contributes toward holding the readers back. Gideon's departing, and preparing the goat, and making the bread, and bringing them to the angel is reported in a mere several seconds, well short of the amount of time it would have taken Gideon to accomplish all these tasks. According to the criteria set out in the section of chapter 5 entitled "Pacing of Events on Time Line," this represents moderate summary material. Further, this follows immediately upon an exchange of direct discourse, representing scene material. Therefore, when Gideon is alone on stage for the first time, constituting a good opportunity for the readers to be drawn into proximity to him, the narrator speeds up the pace, thus providing the readers with a less vivid experience of these actions of Gideon, a move that draws them back to a position at a distance from Gideon on the temporal plane.

In verse 20, the angel is shown giving instructions to Gideon on what he should do with the food he has prepared, and Gideon is shown complying. Because there are two characters on stage again, the *temporal*-plane dynamics analyzed in the preceding paragraph do not help us here, since any manipulation of pacing would draw the readers toward, or away from, both characters at the same time. Still, it is worth noting that Gideon's participation here—actions that would take at least a couple of minutes to accomplish—are afforded a mere two seconds of narrative time with the terse report, "And he did so." Again, when it comes to reporting Gideon's actions, the pace speeds up, depriving the readers of a vivid experience of him.

Verse 21 relates how the angel touches the food with the tip of a staff—causing fire to come up from the rock to consume it—and then vanishes. The fact the angel here vanishes from the scene is, of course, significant to point of view on the *spatial* plane, for the possibility of this character being established as a point-of-view character is now eliminated.

The way in which the angel's disappearance is reported at the end of verse 21 is significant to point of view on the *psychological* plane. Note that in depicting the departure of the angel, the narrator does not simply state the angel vanishes—an objective way of describing it. Rather, the narrator states the angel "went from [Gideon's] eyes." This wording clearly provides the readers with a subjective experience of Gideon; it takes the readers inside Gideon's head for a look out of his eyes at the vanishing visitor. This constitutes an inside view of Gideon, and thus, a dynamic on the psychological plane that has the potential of contributing toward the readers being drawn into proximity to Gideon.

Perspective Criticism

A look at the beginning of verse 22 reveals another inside view of Gideon. The narrator reports, "And Gideon realized it was the angel of Yahweh." The fact that Gideon here comes to realize the visitor is the angel of Yahweh is something to which an objective observer would not be privy; it is something that can be known only through a subjective experience of what is happening inside Gideon's head, and thus, it represents an inside view. Therefore, the inside view of the preceding verse is joined here by another to form a cluster of inside views, and as noted in chapter 3, in the section entitled "Special Considerations in Analyzing Inside Views," clusters of inside views have the effect of drawing the readers into a position of proximity on the *psychological* plane to the character whose inner life is being laid bare.

A move on the *informational* plane of verse 22 also contributes toward drawing the readers into a position in proximity to Gideon. As we have seen, dynamics on this plane have functioned to keep the readers at a distance from Gideon ever since the meeting of Gideon and the angel in verse 12, because the fact that the visitor's identity as the angel of Yahweh has been a part of the information database of the readers, but it has not been a part of the information database of Gideon, thus resulting in a divergence between the databases of the readers and Gideon. However, with Gideon's realization here in verse 22 that the visitor is the angel of Yahweh, that divergence is transformed into a convergence between the databases of the readers and Gideon, and this serves to draw the readers into a position of proximity to Gideon.

Over against these proximity-producing factors, one feature of the psychological-plane dynamics of verse 22 functions to distance the readers from Gideon, namely, the way in which Gideon's realization of his visitor's true identity is presented. It is described by the narrator as follows: "And Gideon said, 'Alas, Adonai Yahweh. For I have seen the angel of Yahweh face to face.'" It is noteworthy this description presents an entirely objective depiction of Gideon's reaction in that it contains nothing beyond what an objective bystander could observe. If the narrator were indeed interested in establishing Gideon as the point-of-view character of this passage, the inclusion of an inside view into his obviously volatile emotional state would be expected here, building on the effect of the two inside views just presented. The fact the narrator does not provide an inside view of Gideon here, but rather, keeps the readers outside of him, suggests an intentional attempt to counteract the effect of the two preceding inside views.

The narrative continues in verses 23–24 with a report of words of assurance from Yahweh to Gideon, and of Gideon building an altar to Yahweh. A *psychological*-plane move to note here is the fact that again the narrator does not supply the readers with an inside view of Gideon's emotional state in response to the words of assurance he has received from Yahweh. He had just been fearing for his life, and so these words of Yahweh would have been life-saving for him. In these circumstances, to have the passage simply continue "... And Gideon built there an altar to Yahweh ..."—with no mention at all of Gideon's emotional reaction to the fact his life has just been spared—comes across as another attempt to keep the readers on the outside of Gideon, and thus, at a distance from him.

With regards to *spatial* positioning, the readers have now encountered fourteen consecutive verses in which Gideon is present, and that much constant exposure to Gideon cannot help but contribute toward the readers' coming to merge with him. However, the constant exposure is abruptly broken in the last part of verse 24 with a notice drawing the readers' attention to the fact the altar Gideon built still stands generations later. This notice functions to rip the readers out of the presence of Gideon; one moment, they are in a position at the side of Gideon, and the next, they have been transported to a time when Gideon is no longer alive. This notice is short, and so, the readers are out of Gideon's presence only momentarily, but the spatial-plane effect of following a particular character for a significant stretch of a narrative is dashed at this point.

Point of view on the *informational* plane is also affected. This notice adds to the readers' information database the fact the altar Gideon built still stands generations later, a fact obviously not a part of the information database of Gideon himself. Therefore, a divergence between the databases of the readers and Gideon is created here, and this also contributes toward the readers being distanced from Gideon.

The *temporal* plane of point of view also reveals evidence of the readers being distanced from Gideon in these verses. In contrast to the scene material reporting pieces of direct discourse of the angel and Gideon in verses 22–23, the report in verse 24 of Gideon building an altar to Yahweh is presented in moderate summary material, in that the time lapse of this action exceeds the length of time it takes to report it by a wide margin. The acceleration of the pace associated with this moderate summary material has the effect of creating within the readers a sense of distance from Gideon.

Perspective Criticism

Verses 25–27 report that Yahweh instructs Gideon to tear down his father's Baal altar and Asherah pole, and build an altar to Yahweh, and that Gideon acts in obedience to these instructions. With regards to point of view on the *spatial* plane, the readers are here returned to a position in proximity to Gideon after having been ripped away from him at the end of verse 24. Further, dynamics on the *informational* plane also contribute toward a sense of proximity, for convergence between the information databases of the readers and Gideon is re-established in this verse, following the brief divergence of databases at the end of verse 24.

With respect to point of view on the *temporal* plane, it is interesting to note the pattern observed in connection to the preceding verses is continued here. The report of an action by Yahweh—the giving of instructions—is given in scene material, whereas the report of an action by Gideon—his taking ten servants and obeying the instructions—is given in moderate summary material. Therefore, Gideon performing an action is again reported with the type of material having the effect of distancing the readers from him.

Point of view on the *psychological* plane is marked by an inside view of Gideon, namely, the narrator's mention of Gideon's motive for acting at night, that is, fear of his family and the townspeople. However, it remains to be seen if there are any subsequent inside views to join together with this one to make an impact on the psychological plane.

Verses 28–31 depict the townspeople discovering Gideon's handiwork from the night before, and demanding his father Joash hand him over to them, with Joash directing them to appeal to Baal to deal with the problem. The material of this segment of the passage exhibits a marked change from all the preceding material. This is most notable on the *spatial* plane, for all this action takes place outside the presence of Gideon. The readers have been positioned in proximity to this character for all but a brief moment since verse 12, but here, they are drawn into the presence of new characters, with Gideon nowhere to be found. Obviously, this functions to distance the readers from Gideon.

The absence of Gideon also has an impact on the *informational* plane of these verses. While all the details reported here are being added to the information database of the readers, they are not being added to the information database of Gideon, since his absence prevents him from being privy to what is happening here. Therefore, a divergence is created between

Old Testament Case Study

the databases of the readers and Gideon, and this serves to distance the readers from Gideon.

Dynamics on the *psychological* plane contribute further toward distancing the readers from Gideon. Verse 28 begins, "The men of the city arose early in the morning, and *behold*! the altar of Baal was torn down." The first clause of this verse simply presents an objective report, depicting the men of the city as mere objects. But then, the narrator inserts the exclamatory "behold!" and this has the effect of having the readers imagine these men all turning their eyes toward the torn-down altar, with the readers following the men's eyes and seeing the torn-down altar through their eyes. This provides for the readers a subjective experience of the men discovering the altar. It must be noted this is the only inside view of the men in this segment of the passage, and so, it does not contribute toward establishing them as a point-of-view group character. However, the fact the readers are being drawn into proximity to these men means the readers are not in proximity to Gideon.

The readers encounter a notice in verse 32 explaining the origins of Gideon's other name, "Jerubbaal," that is, "Let Baal contend against him." Notices of this kind function outside the flow of the storyline of a narrative. With regards to point of view on the *spatial* plane, this means the readers are not here positioned in the midst of the men of the city and Gideon's father, as "Jerubbaal" is established as a new name for Gideon; rather, the establishing of this new name should be understood as taking place in a spatial vacuum, and so, the readers are being distanced here from all the characters present.

The material in verse 33 exhibits another marked change on the *spatial* plane of point of view, a change even more marked than the one experienced at verse 28, for the readers are here ripped completely away from the village which has served as the setting for all the action of the passage to this point. Verse 33 reads, "And all the Midianites and the Amalekites and the people of the east gathered together, and they crossed over and camped in the Valley of Jezreel"; thus, the readers are transported to a position at a distance from Gideon and the townspeople. However, this verse describes the attacking forces in the most general of terms, providing no detail at all of them. As a result, the readers have nothing with which to form pictures of these forces in their mind's eye other than diffuse images of troops in the distance. Therefore, while the readers are here being distanced from

Gideon and the townspeople, they are being kept at a distance from the invading forces as well.

Distance from the invading forces is also created by the dynamics on the *temporal* plane. The report in verse 33 covers not only the gathering of a large number of troops, but also, the movement of all those troops from one location to another, a considerable endeavor requiring a significant amount of time. Yet, a mere several seconds is devoted to the report of these movements, and this moderate summary material speeds up the pace at which the readers are being carried through the events of the passage, thus creating within the readers a sense of distance from these invading forces.

With regards to the *informational* plane of point of view, the activities of the Midianites, Amalekites, and people of east are facts to which Gideon would not be privy. Therefore, the readers are here having information added to their database that puts them in a superior position informationally as compared to Gideon, and this divergence between the information databases of the readers and Gideon functions to contribute further toward distancing the readers from Gideon.

Verses 34–35 report that the spirit of Yahweh comes over Gideon, and he assembles for battle the Abiezrites, and forces from Manasseh, Asher, Zebulun, and Naphtali. On the *informational* plane, convergence is re-established between the information databases of the readers and Gideon as the readers are made privy to the actions of Gideon as he performs them, and this contributes toward the readers moving toward a position of proximity to this character.

On the *spatial* plane also, the readers are transported back toward a position in proximity to Gideon. Note that in contrast to the treatment of the invading forces in the preceding verse, the description of Gideon here does include at least some detail. With regard to his summoning the Abiezrites, the narrator could simply have reported that Gideon "called upon" them, leaving the report bereft of detail. Instead, the narrator states that Gideon "blew on the horn" as his means of summoning them. The inclusion of this detail positions the readers in a spatial location close enough to Gideon to see he is blowing on a horn, creating the image of a character who is not far off in the distance, but rather, in the vicinity of the readers. However, the mention of Gideon's blowing on the horn is not the type of fine detail that would necessitate the readers being right next to Gideon to observe. Therefore, it cannot be concluded yet the readers are here being positioned in proximity to this character.

Old Testament Case Study

Regarding point of view on the *temporal* plane, verses 34–35 constitute more moderate summary material, since the time lapse of Gideon's gathering of his forces far exceeds the time it takes to report these events. Therefore, the pacing here remains fairly fast, thus depriving the readers of the vivid experience of Gideon's actions, which are needed to create within the readers a sense of proximity to him.

Verses 36–37 set out Gideon's first test: asking that a fleece laid out overnight be wet with dew, but the surrounding ground be dry. Proximity to Gideon is created on the *informational* plane, as there is a complete convergence between the information databases of the readers and Gideon at this point. As far as point of view on the *spatial* plane is concerned, the readers are led to follow only Gideon here. On the *temporal* plane, the pace slows right down as the time lapse of this direct discourse equals the length of time needed to report these words; this scene material functions to draw the readers in close on the action, and since Gideon is the only character involved in the action, the readers are drawn in close to him.

The report of the outcome of the test presented in verse 38 reads as follows: "And it was so. He arose early the next day, and squeezed the fleece, and wrung enough dew from the fleece to fill a bowl with water." On the *spatial* plane, the readers continue to follow only Gideon in this verse, and on the *informational* plane, there is still a convergence between the information databases of the readers and Gideon; therefore, the readers are kept in a position of proximity to this character on these two planes.

However, the sense of proximity on the *temporal* plane produced in the preceding verses is not carried over into verse 38. Note that the time lapse of the actions reported here greatly exceeds the amount of time needed to report the actions, as Gideon's rising, going to threshing floor, taking hold of the fleece, and squeezing the water out of it would take much more time than the several seconds needed to report these actions. The loss of vividness resulting from this moderate summary material has the effect of distancing the readers from Gideon.

Dynamics on the *psychological* plane should also be noted. What is striking about the way in which these actions are described is how objectively they are reported. The description simply presents the image of Gideon arising, squeezing a fleece, and wringing water out of it. This is the perspective of a casual bystander who is limited only to observing the outward actions of Gideon, and this has the effect of distancing the readers from this character. It would have been a simple matter for the narrator to provide the readers with more of a subjective experience of Gideon's actions here. For example, the narrator could have reported, "He arose early the next day, and he went and *saw* that the fleece was wet"; the inclusion of something Gideon saw would constitute an inside view, effectively transporting the readers into Gideon's head for a subjective look out through his eyes at the wet fleece. The same subjective experience could have been accomplished with the wording, "He arose early the next day, and *behold!* the fleece was wet," paralleling the inside view of the townspeople in verse 28 in the description of their arising and finding the altar to Baal torn down. However, the narrator employs no such strategy, keeping the readers on the outside of Gideon, thus promoting for them a sense of distance from Gideon.

Verse 39 sets out Gideon's second test—asking that a fleece set out overnight be dry, but the surrounding ground be wet. The sense of proximity to Gideon created on the *spatial* and *informational* planes of the preceding verses continues here, for the readers again follow only Gideon, and their information database remains converged with that of Gideon. And a change on the *temporal* plane results in the readers being brought from a position of distance to a position of proximity, as the moderate summary material of verse 38 gives way to scene material reporting the words of Gideon's pleading with God.

At first glance, it may appear the point-of-view dynamics on all the planes are working together to draw the readers into a position of proximity at this key point in the passage. It must be noted, however, that dynamics on the *psychological* plane of verse 39 still hold the readers at a distance from Gideon. The verse begins, "And Gideon said to God, 'Do not be angry with me...'" These opening words of Gideon's direct discourse clearly reflect an emotional state of anxiety, specifically, a fear of facing the wrath of God. The narrator could have communicated this emotional state by presenting an inside view of Gideon, perhaps by reporting, "And Gideon was afraid ..." Such an incursion into the inner life of Gideon would have been in concert with the dynamics on the spatial, informational, and temporal planes functioning to draw the readers into a position of proximity to Gideon.

However, the narrator does not present Gideon's fear to the readers in this way. Rather, the narrator communicates this fear to the readers only through the words of Gideon's direct discourse, a means that communicates Gideon's fear to the readers *without an inside view*. To put it another way, the narrator informs the readers of this emotional state while keeping them totally outside of Gideon. By doing this, the narrator gets across the fact Gideon is afraid in a way that any objective observer could witness. And the fact the readers are given just this objective experience of Gideon here functions to hold them back from being drawn completely into proximity to him. As a result, the distance produced on the psychological plane of verse 38 is continued here in verse 39.

Verse 40 reports the outcome of the second test: "And God did so that night; it was dry on the fleece only, and on the ground, there was dew." In some ways, this verse is a simple parallel to the report in verse 38 of the outcome of Gideon's first test, only in the reverse; instead of the fleece being wet and the ground being dry, the fleece is now dry and the ground is wet. However, there are some changes from verse 38 that are important to the workings of point of view.

The most significant of these differences occurs on the *spatial* plane. The report of the outcome of the first test recorded in verse 38 reads simply, "And it was so." This report focuses on the resulting state, that is, the fact the conditions for which Gideon asked were indeed present come the morning. The report of the outcome of the second test recorded in verse 40, on the other hand, puts the focus on the fact it is God who brings about the resulting state, and this assertion has the readers following God, as opposed to following Gideon, here at the beginning of the verse. More importantly, whereas verse 38 shows Gideon finding the resulting conditions, verse 40 *makes no mention of Gideon's presence at all* as it reports the resulting conditions of the second test. Therefore, as the readers are reaching the climax of this sequence, they do so out of the presence of Gideon.

The fact Gideon is here removed from the scene also has ramifications for point of view on the *informational* plane. The details presented here are being added to the information database of the readers, but not to the information database of Gideon, thus creating a divergence between the databases of the readers and Gideon, resulting in the readers sensing distance from this character. These dynamics on the informational plane, together with those on the spatial plane, result in the readers losing any sense of proximity to Gideon they had while proceeding through the preceding material as they are pulled to a position distant from him.

Our perspective-critical analysis of this passage has revealed a use of point of view that does not remain constant throughout, but rather, shifts from strategy to strategy. Still, a careful sifting through our findings yields insights that provide a clear indication of how the narrator intends for the readers to evaluate Gideon's actions with the fleece. First, despite the fact the passage as a whole focuses on Gideon, the narrator bypasses the opportunity to introduce the passage with this character, choosing instead to introduce it with the angel, with Gideon only being brought into sight through the angel's point of view. This strongly indicates the narrator is intent on keeping the readers distanced from Gideon. Further, the fact Gideon is kept from realizing the visitor is an angel in verses 12–21 is an informational-plane move fatal to any chance of Gideon being established as a point-of-view character any time during that span of verses, despite the fact the readers' spatial positioning is maintained in proximity to Gideon, as opposed to in proximity to the angel, when the two become separated in verse 19, and the fact the readers are even given an inside view of Gideon at the end of verse 21.

With Gideon's realization in verse 22 that the visitor is an angel, it becomes possible for the first time that he could become established as a point-of-view character, and the narrator's spatial positioning of the readers in proximity to Gideon, together with the provision of another inside view of Gideon in the form of a notice that he "realized" the visitor was an angel, contribute toward that end. However, the narrator's foregoing inside views to lay bare Gideon's emotional state evident in his cry "Alas!" and his inner reaction to discovering he would not be losing his life suggests the narrator is attempting to hold the readers at a distance from Gideon here. And this conclusion is supported by the fact that Gideon's actions reported in verse 24 are only presented in moderate summary material, and by the insertion of the report at the end of the verse having the effect of ripping the readers out of the presence of Gideon.

Verses 25–27 continue to exhibit a balance between proximity-producing and distance-producing moves, with proximity still being promoted on the spatial and informational planes, and distance on the temporal plane. Therefore, there is still a chance even this far into the passage that Gideon could be established as a point-of-view character, though this would require all the moves going forward contribute toward drawing the readers into a position in proximity to this character. However, this does not happen. In fact, the opposite happens as moves on the spatial, informational, temporal, and psychological planes in verses 28–33 contribute toward a distancing of the readers from Gideon. This is fatal to any chance of the readers coming to merge with Gideon by the time of the report of the first test. This being the case, the slight shift back toward proximity to Gideon in verses 34–35 is not able to stem the tide.

Old Testament Case Study

Even the crafting of the material covering Gideon's two tests—the segment of the passage most conducive to having the readers be drawn into proximity to Gideon—exhibits some strong distancing moves. There is the objective nature of the material, completely depriving the readers of even a modicum of a subjective experience of Gideon through these events. But most conclusive is the complete removal of Gideon from the scene in verse 40, right at the climax of the passage.

This overview of the point-of-view contours of this passage should make it clear the readers are *not* being led to merge with Gideon as the point-of-view character of the passage. This is not for a lack of opportunity to do so, for the narrator has at his disposal many point-of-view choices that could have easily accomplished that result. However, the vast majority of them were passed over in favor of choices contributing toward distancing the readers from Gideon.

All this strongly suggests it is the narrator's intention that the readers be established in a position distant from Gideon, for when they witness his two tests with the fleece, and according to point-of-view theory, that has the effect of inclining the readers to disapprove of Gideon's actions. Therefore, it is concluded that in presenting Gideon's two-fold laying out of the fleece, the narrator intends for the readers to disapprove of these actions as a normative means for the discerning of God's will.

Bibliography

Adams, Edward. "Ideology and Point of View in Galatians 1-2: A Critical Linguistic Analysis." In *Diglossia and Other Topics in New Testament Linguistics*, edited by Stanley E. Porter, 205-54. Sheffield, UK: Sheffield Academic Press, 2000.
Alter, Robert. *The Art of Biblical Narrative*. New York: Basic, 1981.
Amit, Yairah. *Reading Biblical Narrative: Literary Criticism and the Hebrew Bible*. Minneapolis: Fortress, 2001.
Andersen, Francis I. *The Sentence in Biblical Hebrew*. The Hague: Mouton, 1974.
Anderson, Janice Capel. *Matthew's Narrative Web: Over, and Over, and Over Again*. Sheffield, UK: Sheffield Academic Press, 1994.
Austen, Jane. *Emma*. Boston: Houghton Mifflin Company, 1957.
Bal, Mieke. *A Mieke Bal Reader*. Chicago: University of Chicago Press, 2006.
Bandstra, Barry L. "Word Order and Emphasis in Biblical Hebrew Narrative: Syntactic Observations on Genesis 22 from a Discourse Perspective." In *Linguistics and Biblical Hebrew*, edited by Walter R. Bodine, 109-23. Winona Lake, IN: Eisenbrauns, 1992.
Bar-Efrat, Shimon. *Narrative Art in the Bible*. Translated by Dorothea Shefer-Vanson. Sheffield, UK: Almond, 1989.
Berlin, Adele. *Poetics and Interpretation of Biblical Narrative*. Winona Lake, IN: Eisenbrauns, 1994.
———. "Point of View in Biblical Narrative." In *A Sense of Text: The Act of Language in the Study of Biblical Narrative*, edited by S. A. Geller, 171-87. Winona Lake, IN: Eisenbrauns, 1982.
Blass, F., and A. Debrunner. *A Greek Grammar of the New Testament and Other Early Christian Literature*. Translated by Robert W. Funk. Chicago: University of Chicago Press, 1961.
Block, Daniel L. "Will the Real Gideon Please Stand Up? Narrative Style and Intention in Judges 6-9." *Journal of the Evangelical Theological Society* 40 (1997) 353-66.
Booth, Wayne. *The Rhetoric of Fiction*. 2nd ed. Chicago: University of Chicago Press, 1983.
Chatman, Seymour. *Story and Discourse: Narrative Structure in Fiction and Film*. Ithaca, NY: Cornell University Press, 1978.
Conroy, Charles. *Absalom Absalom! Narrative and Language in 2 Sam 13-20*. Rome: Biblical Institute Press, 1978.
Culpepper, R. Alan. *Anatomy of the Fourth Gospel: A Study in Literary Design*. Philadelphia: Fortress, 1983.
Darr, John A. *On Character Building: The Reader and the Rhetoric of Characterization in Luke-Acts*. Louisville: Westminster John Knox, 1992.
Dewey, Joanna. "Point of View and the Disciples in Mark." In *SBL 1982 Seminar Papers*, edited by Kent Harold Richards, 97-106. Chico, CA: Scholars, 1982.

Bibliography

du Rand, J. S. "Plot and Point of View in the Gospel of John." In *A South African Perspective on the New Testament*, edited by J. H. Petzer and P. J. Hartin, 149–69. Leiden: Brill, 1986.

Fokkelman, J. P. *Narrative Art in Genesis: Specimens of Stylistic and Structural Analysis*. Assen: Koninklijke Van Gorcum, 1975.

———. *Reading Biblical Narrative: An Introductory Guide*. Translated by Ineke Smit. Louisville, KY: Westminster John Knox, 1999.

Fowler, Roger. *Linguistics and the Novel*. London: Methuen, 1977.

———. *Linguistic Criticism*. 2nd ed. Oxford: Oxford University Press, 1996.

Friedman, Norman. "Point of View in Fiction: The Development of a Critical Concept." *Publications of the Modern Language Association of America* 70 (1955) 1160–84.

Genette, Gérard. *Narrative Discourse: An Essay in Method*. Translated by Jane E. Lewin. Ithaca, NY: Cornell University Press, 1980.

Goldfajn, Tal. *Word Order and Time in Biblical Hebrew Narrative*. Oxford: Clarendon, 1998.

Gowler, David B. *Host, Guest, Enemy, and Friend: Portraits of the Pharisees in Luke and in Acts*. New York: Lang, 1991.

Grabo, Carl H. *The Technique of the Novel*. New York: Gordian, 1928.

Haacker, K. "Einige Falle von 'erlebter Rede' im Neuen Testament." *Novum Testamentum* 12 (1970) 70–77.

Halliday, M. A. K. "Linguistic Function and Literary Style: An Inquiry into the Language of William Golding's 'The Inheritors.'" In *Essays in Modern Stylistics*, edited by Donald C. Freeman, 325–60. London: Methuen, 1981.

James, Henry. "The Art of Fiction." In *Henry James: The Future of the Novel*, edited by Leon Edel, 3–27. New York: Vintage, 1956.

Katz, Steven D. *Film Directing Shot by Shot: Visualizing from Concept to Screen*. Studio City, CA: Wiese Productions, 1991.

Kingsbury, Jack Dean. "The Figure of Jesus in Matthew's Story: A Literary-Critical Probe." *Journal for the Study of the New Testament* 21 (1984) 3–36.

———. *Matthew as Story*. 2nd ed. Philadelphia: Fortress, 1988.

Kuno, Susumu. *Functional Syntax: Anaphora, Discourse and Empathy*. Chicago: University of Chicago Press, 1987.

Kuno, Susumu, and Etsuko Kaburaki. "Empathy and Syntax." *Linguistic Inquiry* 8 (1977) 627–72.

Lanser, Susan Sniader. *The Narrative Act: Point of View in Prose Fiction*. Princeton: Princeton University Press, 1981.

Leech, Geoffrey N., and Michael H. Short. *Style in Fiction: A Linguistic Introduction to English Fictional Prose*. London: Longman, 1981.

Licht, Jacob. *Storytelling in the Bible*. Jerusalem: Magnes, 1978.

Lotman, J. M. "Point of View in a Text." *New Literary History* 6 (1975) 339–52.

Lubbock, Percy. *The Craft of Fiction*. London: Jonathan Cape, 1921.

Lyons, William John. "The Words of Gamaliel (Acts 5.38–39) and the Irony of Indeterminacy." *Journal for the Study of the New Testament* 68 (1997) 23–49.

Macelli, Joseph V. *The Five C's of Cinematography: Motion Picture Filming Techniques*. Los Angeles: Silman-James, 1965.

Malbon, Elizabeth Struthers. *Mark's Jesus: Characterization as Narrative Christology*. Waco, TX: Baylor University Press, 2009.

Bibliography

Meadowcroft, Tim. "Point of View in Storytelling: An Experiment in Narrative Criticism in Daniel 4." *Didaskalia* 8.2 (1997) 30–42.

Merenlahti, Petri. *Poetics for the Gospels? Rethinking Narrative Criticism.* Edinburgh: T. & T. Clark, 2002.

Moore, Stephen D. *Literary Criticism and the Gospels: the Theoretical Challenge.* New Haven: Yale University Press, 1989.

Nelson, Richard D. "The Anatomy of the Book of Kings." *Journal for the Study of the Old Testament* 40 (1988) 39–48.

Nida, Eugene. "Implications of Contemporary Linguistics for Biblical Scholarship." *Journal of Biblical Literature* 91 (1972) 73–89.

Olsson, Birger. *Structure and Meaning in the Fourth Gospel: A Text-Linguistic Analysis of John 2:1–11 and 4:1–42.* Translated by Jean Grey. Lund: CSK Gleerup, 1974.

Parsons, Mikeal Carl. *The Departure of Jesus in Luke-Acts: The Ascension Narratives in Context.* Sheffield, UK: Sheffield Academic Press, 1987.

Perry, Menahem, and Meir Sternberg. "The King through Ironic Eyes: Biblical Narrative and the Literary Reading Process." *Poetics Today* 7 (1986) 275–322.

Petersen, Norman R. "'Point of View' in Mark's Narrative." *Semeia* 12 (1978) 97–121.

Polzin, Robert. *Moses and the Deuteronomist: A Literary Study of the Deuteronomic History.* New York: Seabury, 1980.

Porter, Stanley E. "Word Order and Clause Structure in New Testament Greek: An Unexplored Area of Greek Linguistics Using Philippians as a Test Case." *Filologia Neotestamentaria* 6 (1993) 177–205.

Powell, Mark Allan. "Direct and Indirect Phraseology in the Gospel of Matthew." In *SBL 1991 Seminar Papers*, edited by Eugene H. Lovering, 405–17. Atlanta: Scholars, 1991.

———. "The Plot to Kill Jesus from Three Different Perspectives: Point of View in Matthew." In *SBL 1990 Seminar Papers*, edited by David J. Lull, 603–13. Atlanta: Scholars, 1990.

Resseguie, James L. "Point of View in the Central Section of Luke (9:51—19:44)." *Journal of the Evangelical Theological Society* 25 (1982) 41–47.

———. *The Strange Gospel: Narrative Design and Point of View in John.* Leiden: Brill, 2001.

Rhoads, David, et al. *Mark as Story: An Introduction to the Narrative of a Gospel.* 2nd ed. Minneapolis: Fortress, 1999.

Scholes, Robert, and Robert Kellogg. *The Nature of Narrative.* New York: Oxford University Press, 1966.

Scott, Bernard Brandon. *Hear Then the Parable: A Commentary on the Parables of Jesus.* Minneapolis: Fortress, 1989.

Simpson, Paul. *Language, Ideology, and Point of View.* London: Routledge, 1993.

Staley, Jeffrey Lloyd. *The Print's First Kiss: A Rhetorical Investigation of the Implied Reader in the Fourth Gospel.* Atlanta: Scholars, 1988.

Stanzel, F. K. *A Theory of Narrative.* Translated by Charlotte Goedsche. Cambridge: Cambridge University Press, 1984.

Sternberg, Meir. *The Poetics of Biblical Narrative: Ideological Literature and the Drama of Reading.* Bloomington, IN: Indiana University Press, 1985.

Szeman, Sherri. *Mastering Point of View.* Cincinnati: Story, 2001.

Tannehill, Robert C. "The Disciples in Mark: The Function of a Narrative Role." *Journal of Religion* 57 (1977) 386–405.

Bibliography

———. *The Narrative Unity of Luke-Acts: A Literary Interpretation.* Vol. 1, *The Gospel according to Luke.* Philadelphia: Fortress, 1986.

Toolan, Michael. *Narrative: A Critical Linguistic Introduction.* 2nd ed. London: Routledge, 2001.

Tovey, Derek. *Narrative Art and Act in the Fourth Gospel.* Sheffield, UK: Sheffield Academic Press, 1997.

Turnell, Martin. "Madame Bovary." In *Flaubert: A Collection of Critical Essays,* edited by Raymond Giraud, 97–111. Englewood Cliffs, NJ: Prentice-Hall, 1964.

Uspensky, Boris. *A Poetics of Composition: The Structure of the Artistic Text and Typology of a Compositional Form.* Translated by Valentina Zavarin and Susan Wittig. Berkeley: University of California Press, 1973.

Van Aarde, A. G. "Narrative Criticism Applied to John 4:43–54." In *Text and Interpretation: New Approaches in the Criticism of the New Testament,* edited by P. J. Hartin and J. H. Petzer, 101–28. Leiden: Brill, 1991.

Weimann, Robert. *Structure and Society in Literary History: Studies in the History and Theory of Historical Criticism.* Charlottesville, VA: University Press of Virginia, 1976.

Yamasaki, Gary. *John the Baptist in Life and Death: Audience-Oriented Criticism of Matthew's Narrative.* Sheffield, UK: Sheffield Academic Press, 1998.

———. "Point of View in a Gospel Story: What Difference Does It Make? Luke 19:1–10 as a Test Case." *Journal of Biblical Literature* 125 (2006) 89–105.

———. *Watching a Biblical Narrative: Point of View in Biblical Exegesis.* London: T. & T. Clark, 2007.

Scripture Index

Old Testament

Genesis
8:8–12	64
21:9–21	96
32:3–30	107
32:3–5	107
32:3–6	107
32:6	107
32:7a	108
32:7–8	107
32:9–12	107
32:13–21	107
32:20a	108
32:22–23	107
32:24–30	107

Exodus
4:1–9	49
4:3	49
4:3b–4	49
4:6	49
4:6b–7	49

Numbers
11:31	32

Joshua
9:3–13	65
9:14–15	65

10:1	50
10:2	50

Judges
6	1
6–9	140
6:11	142
6:11–12a	141
6:12a	141
6:12	142, 144, 146
6:12–21	152
6:12b–18	141, 142
6:14	142
6:16	142
6:19	142, 143, 152
6:20	143
6:21	143, 152
6:22	144, 152
6:22–23	145
6:23–24	145
6:24	145, 146, 152
6:25–27	146, 152
6:28	147, 150
6:28–31	146
6:28–33	152
6:32	147
6:33	147, 148
6:34–35	148, 149, 152
6:36–37	149
6:36–40	140
6:38	149, 150, 151
6:39	150, 151

Scripture Index

Judges (*cont.*)

6:40	151, 153
13:1–24	56
13:3	56
13:6	56
13:7	56
13:8	56
13:11–16a	56
13:16b	56
13:19	56
13:20	56
13:21b	57
19:1	114
19:1–21	114
19:2	114
19:3	114
19:3–9	114
19:5–8	114
19:10–15	114
19:16–21	114

Ruth

2:1	48
2:4	48
4:1	48
4:1–12	48

1 Samuel

9:3–14	25
9:14	25

1 Kings

10:1	42
11:6	6
14:5	85
14:7–16	85
16:8–28	78
17:8–10a	81
17:8–16	81
17:10b	81
17:10c–11	82
19:11–12	82

2 Kings

5:1–19a	21
5:2–3	21
5:4–5a	22
5:5b–7	22
5:8	22
5:9–10	22
5:11–13	22
5:14	22
5:15–19a	22
7:3–7	75
7:6–7	75

1 Chr

10:1	88, 89
10:1–6	88
10:2	89
10:3	89
10:4–5	89

Esther

1:10–12	40
1:12b	40
6:1–12	116
6:6	116

Jonah

4:5a	80
4:5–8	79
4:5b	80
4:5c	80
4:6	80
4:6–11	79n10
4:7	80
4:8a	80
4:8b	80
4:9–11	80

Scripture Index

NEW TESTAMENT

Matthew

2:7–12	50
2:8	50
2:9	50
2:10	51
2:11a	51
3:17	68
5:3—7:27	73
13:58	61
14:1–2	61
14:1–12	61
14:3–12	61
15:1	27
17:5	68
19:16–21	84
19:16	84
19:17	84
19:18–19	84
19:20	84
19:21	84
21:14	26
27:40	68

Mark

1:9—14:50	21
3:1–5	108
3:3–5	108
5:25	58
5:26	58
6:5	61
6:14–29	21
6:45–52	38
7:1–8	86
7:3–4	86
7:5	86
9:2	46
9:2–8	46
9:3	62
9:4	46
9:14	33
16:5	61

Luke

5:8	94
5:12	95
7:6	95
7:13	95n5
7:19	95n5
9:28–36	46
9:29	47
9:30	47
9:32b	46
10:1	95n5
10:39	95n5
10:41	95n5
11:39	95n5
12:35–40	95
12:41	95
12:41–42	95
12:42	95, 95n5, 96
13:15	95n5
17:5	95n5
17:6	95n5
18:6	95n5
19:1–4	44
19:1–10	44, 110
19:2	111
19:4	111
19:5	44, 111
19:8	95n5
22:61	95n5
24:51	9

John

2:13–22	77
2:19	77
2:21	77
2:22	77
3:14–15	104
3:16	105n20
5:24	105

Scripture Index

John (cont.)

6:40	105
6:47	105
7:1	40
19:19	66
20:1–2	72
20:31	105
21:15–17a	72
21:17b	72

Acts

4:1–18	130
4:19–20	130
4:36–37	28
5:12–16	131
5:17	131, 134
5:17–18	131, 132
5:17–24	138
5:18	132
5:18–21a	133
5:19–21a	132, 134, 137
5:21b	133
5:21b–24	132, 137
5:21b–25	133
5:22	133, 134, 135
5:25	135
5:25–26	133, 134, 137
5:25–34	138
5:26	133, 134, 135
5:27–32	135, 138
5:33	136
5:33–34	136, 138
5:34	130, 139
5:35–39	128
9:1–9	30
9:8	30
9:20–25	28
9:26–27	28
9:28–29	28
10:9–16	52
10:11	52
11:22	28
11:22–23	86
11:22–24	86
11:24a	86
11:25–26	28
11:27–30	27
11:30	27, 28
12:25	27, 28
13:2	28n18
13:7	27, 28
15:1–21	32
15:7a	32
15:7b–11	32
15:12	32
15:13–21	32
15:36–40	13

Movie Index

Adaptation, 37–38
All the President's Men, 63–64
Apocalypse Now, 20–21
Around the World in 80 Days, 101
Avatar, 99–101

Beautiful Mind, A, 36
Bridge on the River Kwai, The, 102–103
Butch Cassidy and the Sundance Kid, 13–17, 107, 117–27

Casablanca, 112–14
Citizen Kane, 29–30
Close Encounters of the Third Kind, 51–52
Crouching Tiger Hidden Dragon, 57–58

Daredevil, 41–42
Dark Knight, The, 66
Das Boot, 20

E.T.: The Extra-Terrestrial, 115–16

Gallipoli, 85–86
Godfather, The, 38
Gods Must be Crazy, The, 2–4, 6, 93–94, 95
Gone With the Wind, 39

Jaws, 87–88
Jesus Christ Superstar, 76–77
Jesus Film, 9

Jurassic Park, 43–44
Lady in the Lake, 45–46
Lawrence of Arabia, 18–19, 28–29

Memento, 59–61
Mr. Holland's Opus, 41
My Fair Lady, 92

Psycho, 83–84

Raiders of the Lost Ark, 47–48
Rocky, 79

Seven Samurai, 32
Shakespeare in Love, 66–68
Shawshank Redemption, The, 37n2
Shrek, 109–10
Slumdog Millionaire, 74–75
Star Wars: Revenge of the Sith, 92–93
Sting, The, 65
Stranger Than Fiction, 4–5

Terminator, The, 98–99
Thelma and Louise, 24–25
Titanic, 33
Truman Show, The, 7–8
Twelve Angry Men, 31–32

Up, 78
Usual Suspects, The, 71–72

WALL-E, 101-2
Witness for the Prosecution, 70–71
Wizard of Oz, The, 80–81

www.ingramcontent.com/pod-product-compliance
Lightning Source LLC
Chambersburg PA
CBHW030858170426
43193CB00009BA/659